GROWING POINTS IN THEOLOGY

PROPHECY AND TRADITION

Also in this series:

PROPHECY AND TRADITION

R. E. CLEMENTS

University Lecturer in Divinity and
Fellow of Fitzwilliam College, Cambridge

JOHN KNOX PRESS
ATLANTA, GEORGIA

LIBRARY OF CONGRESS CATALOGING IN PUBLICATION DATA

Clements, Ronald Ernest, 1929–
  Prophecy and tradition.

  (Growing points in theology)
  Bibliography: p.
  1. Prophets. I. Title.
BS1198.C57 1975   221.1'5   74-3713
ISBN 0-8042-0110-2

Printed in Great Britain by
The Camelot Press Ltd, Southampton

Contents

Abbreviations

BA	*The Biblical Archaeologist*
BASOR	*Bulletin of the American Schools of Oriental Research*
BKAT	Biblischer Kommentar. Altes Testament
BWANT	Beiträge zur Wissenschaft vom Alten und Neuen Testament
BZAW	Beihefte zur Zeitschrift für die alttestamentliche Wissenschaft
CBQ	*Catholic Biblical Quarterly*
EvTh	*Evangelische Theologie*
FRLANT	Forschungen zur Religion und Literatur des Alten und Neuen Testaments
JBL	*Journal of Biblical Literature*
JNES	*Journal of Near Eastern Studies*
SBT	Studies in Biblical Theology
SEÅ	*Svenskt exegetisk Årsbok*
SVT	Supplements to Vetus Testamentum
ThB	Theologische Bücherei
ThSt	Theologische Studien
ThZ	*Theologische Zeitschrift*
VT	*Vetus Testamentum*
WMANT	Wissenschaftliche Monographien zum Alten und Neuen Testaments
ZAW	*Zeitschrift für die alttestamentliche Wissenschaft*
ZThK	*Zeitschrift für Theologie und Kirche*

I

Introduction

The study of the relationship of the Old Testament prophets to tradition, understood broadly as the wide context of historical, institutional, and liturgical traditions of Israel's religion which they received, used, and in some cases rejected, has come to form a major aspect of recent studies of the Old Testament prophets. This has undoubtedly been brought into sharpest focus by the illuminating treatment of the prophets by G. von Rad in his *Old Testament Theology, Vol. II, The Theology of Israel's Prophetic Traditions*,[1] but it has inevitably been forced upon scholars by a whole range of reassessments of the traditions of Israel's religion. The understanding of prophetic originality among earlier scholars had led to a considerable underestimating of the importance of the place of tradition in the prophets' preaching, and the redressing of the balance in this rightly represents a 'growing point' of Old Testament study. Furthermore, the insights of form criticism, traditio-historical criticism, and redaction criticism have all led to a much deeper awareness of particular dimensions in which the prophets could reveal their indebtedness to tradition, so that with the help of these methods a fuller understanding of the prophets is attainable. Understandably, both these methods and conclusions about the prophetic preaching based upon them, have at times produced some quite startling and extreme presentations. Inevitably also there have been voices of protest that such interpretations obscure the originality and individuality of the prophet's own voice, and reduce him simply to the level of a mouthpiece of much older ideas and conventions. These protests are not without their own value, and the general title, 'prophets and tradition', should not be taken to indicate that the aim of this study is to

[1] Eng. Tr., Edinburgh and London, 1965.

endeavour to establish the claim that the prophets were so
decisively dependent upon tradition that their own originality
was lost to it.

It is in any case important to recognize at the outset that
influence can be exercised in different ways, sometimes positively
and affirmatively, and at others negatively. In fact, there is an
immense number of ways in which the influence of a tradition
may be felt, either consciously or unconsciously, so that even
views which regard the prophets as reacting violently against the
traditions of worship and piety which they received are very
decidedly concerned with the question of prophecy and tradition.
Thus the arguments which were widely held in the earlier part of
this century regarding the sharp rejection by the prophets of the
traditions of worship and sacrifice which were current in the Israel
of their day must certainly be regarded as arguments about the
prophets and tradition. The subject itself is not new, therefore,
even though it has come to enjoy a new prominence as deserving
of special, and independent, attention. What is particularly new
is a deepening awareness that such a sharp conflict with tradition,
and such a negative attitude towards it, does not characterize the
prophets throughout, however valid it is at certain points. Furthermore, there can be no doubt that, in the past, scholarship has
sometimes found conflicts where none existed, or has wrongly
credited the prophets with originating ideas and attitudes which
they in fact inherited. Perhaps most of all the tendency to class
the great classical prophets of the Old Testament as 'opposition
prophets' because of their opposition to the older religion of
Israel has encouraged the view that they were, by virtue of their
calling, destined to oppose the piety and religious institutions of
their day. The result has sometimes been that very little clear
attention has been directed to what it was exactly that the prophets opposed and why. Thus, to cite the most striking example,
the prophetic opposition to sacrifice has been regarded as a straightforward instance of their opposition to man's attempts to appease
God by his own religious good works. The many and varied
expressions of criticism of sacrifice in the Psalms, Proverbs, and
Historical Books of the Old Testament have been regarded as
deriving from this basic prophetic opposition to man's attempts to
save himself from God's wrath. Yet, in fact, the reasons presented
in the Old Testament for opposing certain sacrificial acts, or
certain ways of understanding them, are so varied that it is highly

improbable that they all derive from a common basic insight. No uniformity of criticism is apparent here, and it is extremely improbable, therefore, that the prophets can be held to have been responsible for initiating such criticism. To what extent the prophets themselves inherited traditions critical of certain types of worship is far from clear, and is a subject well worth examining. Undoubtedly, therefore, the prophets cannot be adequately characterized as 'opposition prophets' as though opposition to existing institutions was the basis of their calling. This is not to deny, however, that they were forced into a very sharp opposition to the political and religious leadership of their day. How far tradition played a part in this, and how far such a clash created a new kind of tradition concerning the role of the prophets, and also concerning the ideal of political government and religious leadership that Israel should have, is a part of our general concern.

That prophecy created distinctive traditions of its own, which could in retrospect be looked at together as forming a kind of unified prophetic tradition, should not be denied. We can discern recognizable similarities between the very earliest prophets mentioned in the Old Testament, such as Balaam, as well as those who appear in connection with Saul and David, and the later canonical prophets both in their activity and in the characteristics of their preaching. Yet this prophetic tradition was not a self-contained entity, cut off from other branches of Israel's religious life. Originally, each prophet belonged to a particular age so that his preaching was very directly bound up with the contemporary religious scene. In this regard we can discern in certain of the canonical prophets a dependence on particular predecessors among the prophets, e.g. Ezekiel upon Jeremiah and Jeremiah upon Hosea. Yet prophecy did not flow entirely in channels of its own making, but expressed itself in connection with a wide range of other features of Israel's religious and national existence; the cultus, the court and institutions of family and tribal society.

Viewed in the light of these considerations, the study of prophecy and tradition becomes an inescapable part of the task of interpreting the prophets in their own contemporary setting. This means not only studying them against the background of the general political and historical circumstances in which they were active, and to which in part they addressed themselves, but also viewing them in the light of the religious ideas and practices which they received. Thereby we can see that their preaching represented a kind of internal dialogue within Israel in which a number of accepted ideas and institutions were subjected to a searching scrutiny. The sequel to this dialogue is to be found in the rise of Judaism, when many of the old institutions of Israel disappeared, and others were modified often in a very radical way. Thus the study of this prophetic dialogue with tradition has far-reaching implications for an understanding of how the Jews came to be the people of a book. Eventually, by the time the temple of Jerusalem was destroyed in A.D. 70, very few of the old religious institutions of Israel were left. None the less, Judaism continued, and held as a foundation of its existence a commitment to the canonical scriptures which included the Former and the Latter Prophets. These prophets had preached a message about God and his people which had become central to an understanding of their relationship. In this way the prophetic writings became part of the tradition of a reborn Israel. The subject of prophecy and tradition therefore does not end with the words spoken by the prophets, but continues on to examine how the prophetic words became part of a new tradition—the tradition of a book and of the people of this book.

In this regard it is important to note that our English word 'tradition' can be used in different senses. The first of these refers to the process of 'handing on', and is concerned with the activity of transmission by which the words of a folk-tale, a legend, a psalm, or a prophecy were handed on to subsequent generations (cf. the German *Überlieferungsgeschichte*, properly 'transmission history'). The study of this process of transmission must necessarily look at the circumstances, methods, and circles by which the original material was preserved and adapted until it reached its present literary form. It is this sense of the word tradition that is uppermost in S. Mowinckel's study *Prophecy and Tradition: The Prophetic Books in the Light of the Study of the Growth and History of the Tradition*,[2] where he is primarily concerned with the process of transmission by which the words which the prophets originally spoke were eventually redacted into written form in books. Alongside this use of the word 'tradition' we must set its use in reference to the content of what is handed on, and thus more broadly to a whole range of customs, ideas, and conventions which are 'handed on' in a society (cf. the German *Traditionsgeschichte*—'tradition history'). In Old Testament study this has come to refer to the

[2] Oslo, 1946.

isolation and analysis of particular traditions, or themes, which enjoyed a long historical development in Israel, and which were especially related to specific localities, institutions, or circles within the nation. The prophets were influenced by these traditions through historical or geographical association, or through a particular religious identification of some kind, so that their preaching sometimes marks a stage in the history of the development of a tradition. Furthermore the recognition of a familiarity with specific traditions has been employed to formulate hypotheses about the special religious and cultural background of certain prophets, which have then in turn been used as the basis for a general guide to the religious and spiritual content of the situations in which they preached. In some cases, as for example in von Rad's treatment of Isaiah against the background of the 'Zion tradition' of the Jerusalem cult, this has been particularly illuminating.[3]

In practice these different meanings of the word 'tradition' soon begin to pass into one another, and the method of research known as 'tradition history' inevitably becomes concerned with both of them. Whilst we can clearly make a distinction between 'tradition', understood as the process of transmitting the prophets' words, and 'tradition' as indicating the themes and customs which influenced a prophet when he preached, there is an inevitable area of overlap. Thus it must be borne in mind that if the preaching of a prophet shows that he was strongly influenced by his association with Jerusalem, as in the case of Isaiah, then not only will his preaching have been affected by features current in the religious life of the city, but the subsequent transmission of his words will also almost certainly have been affected by this background. Thus the particular character of the religious life of the city will probably have affected the transmission of the prophet's words in ways not unlike those in which it influenced the prophet himself. Furthermore, the particular context in which a prophecy was given inevitably established a certain range of possibilities for the manner and method of its transmission. In many cases, therefore, the evidence of familiarity with a particular tradition in a prophetic book may

[3] G. von Rad, *Old Testament Theology*, Vol. II, pp. 155 ff., and also his essay 'The City on the Hill', *The Problem of the Hexateuch and Other Essays*, Edinburgh and London, 1965, pp. 232–42. For the influence of the Jerusalem cult on a prophet, we may also cf. G. W. Ahlström, *Joel and the Temple Cult of Jerusalem* (SVT 21), Leiden, 1971.

be quite variously interpreted. It may be taken to be an indication of a theme or custom which influenced the prophet's preaching, or it may simply be regarded as a pointer to the circles and influences which affected the transmission of the prophet's words. The reader will readily discern that old and familiar controversies about authentic and inauthentic sayings of the prophets arise here and cannot be ignored. It is to be borne in mind, nevertheless, that the question of the concern of the prophets with tradition moves in two directions: it concerns the presence and use of traditional themes and motifs in the prophets' preaching, and also the processes by which the original prophetic sayings were developed into our present books. If the former concern is most to the fore in what has come to be called 'traditio-historical method', the latter processes are very much the subject of examination in 'redaction criticism'. Both methods presuppose a familiarity with, and use of, form criticism, so that each method examines particular aspects of the content and structure of our extant prophetic literature, and there is a good deal of overlap between them.

What is fundamental to a redactio-critical approach to the prophetic books is the attempt to understand and interpret the form and intention of these books as a whole. This means both a study of the form and arrangement of the whole book, comprising primary and secondary material, and also a careful appraisal of the structure of the larger units of which the books are composed. It may at times look at the ordering and conjunction of quite short sayings and oracles with a view to discerning in their formal arrangement some clue as to the intention of the editors who have made this arrangement. The knowledge of this intention can then help us very considerably in two ways. It can serve as some guide to the way in which the editor interpreted the original prophetic sayings, thereby becoming our earliest pointer to what the prophet was believed to have meant. It can also point to those interests which led to the inclusion of the prophetic writings in the Old Testament canon, thereby showing us something of the significance which was attached to their preservation.

Such a redactio-critical approach does not dispense with a literary-critical study, although it frequently moves in another direction. Whereas literary criticism divides authentic from inauthentic material, it tends too readily to dismiss the latter as of only slight relevance. In fact, however, as redaction criticism seeks to show, this 'inauthentic' material frequently serves as a development and interpretation of the original prophetic saying. Furthermore, redaction criticism is sometimes able to show that apparently contradictory sayings of a prophet may be brought together by an editor for a special purpose. Viewed in their original historical context such sayings may not have been as contradictory as their present literary conjunction would suggest. This particularly applies to the tensions inherent in the cyclic arrangement of threats of doom with promises of divine help and restoration. Thus although form criticism, tradition criticism, and redaction criticism presuppose and build upon a basic literary criticism, they frequently lead to an understanding of the prophetic literature which is very different from the earlier purely literary-critical approach. The newer methods add a dimension of depth which rejects any too sharp contrast between authentic and inauthentic sayings of the prophets. Rather they see that these sayings were originally spoken within the context of an already established prophetic tradition, and themselves became the basis of a development which sought to clarify, interpret and apply what the prophets had said to later ages. To ignore the tradition which stemmed from the prophets' original sayings is to cut loose from the strongest guidelines that we have to what those sayings really meant. With an interest in these new methods, therefore, we can proceed to look at several aspects of the relationship between the Old Testament prophets and tradition.

2

The Prophets and the Covenant

Within the Old Testament the most important circle of traditions which may be expected to have influenced Israel's prophets are those which concern the covenant relationship between Yahweh and Israel. Since this covenant relationship was not centred in one single tradition, but utilized various tradition elements concerning Israel's origin, and since these covenant traditions of Israel are very wide-ranging in their implications and have been very differently interpreted by different scholars, it is necessary to restrict the scope of the present chapter. The problems concerning the interpretation of the divine covenant between God and Israel are well surveyed by D. J. McCarthy,[1] and some of the material of relevance to the prophets was surveyed earlier in my monograph, *Prophecy and the Covenant*.[2] In our present examination, therefore, it may be sufficient to look only at the two most influential interpretations of covenant which have been current in recent study of the Old Testament, and to consider the ways in which traditions relating to them have been thought to be reflected in the prophets. The first of these concerns the hypothesis that the pre-monarchic structure of Israel as a federation of twelve tribes was organized as an amphictyony with its worship focused upon a central sanc-

[1] D. J. McCarthy, *Old Testament Covenant. A Survey of Current Opinions*, Oxford, 1972. For a general introduction to the subject, cf. also D. R. Hillers, *Covenant. The History of a Biblical Idea*, Baltimore, 1970, and K. Baltzer, *The Covenant Formulary*, Oxford, 1971. A much more critical estimate of the prevalence of covenant ideas in the Old Testament is presented by L. Perlitt, *Bundestheologie im Alten Testament* (WMANT 36), Neukirchen, 1969. Cf. also E. Kutsch, *Verheissung und Gesetz* (BZAW 131), Berlin, 1973.

[2] *Prophecy and Covenant* (SBT 43), London, 1965.

tuary to which all the tribes contributed and in which they shared.[3] The second prevalent hypothesis about Israel's covenant concerns its form, which, it has been argued, was an adaptation of the form of ancient Near Eastern Suzerainty treaties.[4] Both hypotheses have led to distinctive interpretations of the prophets centring upon the use made by them of older traditions associated with Israel's covenant.

The hypothesis regarding the structure of pre-monarchic Israel as an amphictyony has led to the attempt to establish the hypothesis of the existence in the nation of a distinctive prophetic 'office' to which several of the great classical prophets are thought to have belonged. Such a prophetic 'office', it is argued, originated in the amphictyony where a central 'law speaker' fulfilled the role of guardian of the sacred traditions of law which governed the conduct of the tribes. Such a 'law speaker' held an office which carried an obligation towards all Israel, and was thereby representative not simply of the local traditions of any one tribe. Further, he may be regarded as having acted as a mediator between Yahweh and Israel in a way that no other single person could have emulated before the introduction of the monarchy. This hypothesis of the existence of a covenant mediator has been built up largely around the claim of A. Alt that such figures may be reflected in the lists of minor judges in the Old Testament (Ju. 10:3–5; 12:8–15),[5] and that these minor judges had something to do with the preservation and proclamation of apodictic law in Israel. From this there have been built up interpretations which suggest that the Pentateuchal traditions about the work of Moses may have developed out of a recollection of this mediating office of the amphictyony, and that in a later age certain great prophets may have regarded their work as reviving and fulfilling this ancient role.[6] For the moment we may leave aside the question of how strongly this

[3] Cf. M. Noth, *Das System der Zwölf Stämme Israels* (BWANT IV: 1), Stuttgart, 1930; *The History of Israel*, 2nd ed., 1960, pp. 85 ff.

[4] So especially G. E. Mendenhall, 'Ancient Oriental and Biblical Law', *BA* 17 (1954), pp. 26–46; 'Covenant Forms in Israelite Tradition', *BA* 17 (1954), pp. 50–76, and his article 'Covenant', *IDB* I, 714–23.

[5] A. Alt, 'The Origins of Israelite Law', *EOTHR*, pp. 102–3; cf. also M. Noth, 'Das Amt des "Richters Israels"', *Ges. Stud. zum A.T.*, II, Munich, 1969, pp. 71–85, esp. pp. 81 f.

[6] So especially H. J. Kraus, *Die prophetische Verkündigung des Rechts in Israel* (TS 51), Zürich–Zollikon, 1957, pp. 11 ff.; H. Graf Reventlow, 'Prophetenamt und Mittleramt?' *ZThK* 58 (1961), pp. 269–84.

reconstruction of the role of a pre-monarchic covenant mediator
is supported from the Old Testament evidence, and be content to
note that the whole hypotheis of an amphictyony has come under
very sharp and searching criticism in recent studies.[7] Furthermore,
this criticism has particularly drawn attention to the very hypothetical nature of attempts to reconstruct the outlines of certain
institutions and traditions which are claimed to have belonged to
such an amphictyony. So far as the prophets are concerned the
amphictyonic hypothesis has been brought in primarily in connection with the Deuteronomic interpretation of the role of the
prophet as a continuation of the office of Moses. This is to be
found in the Deuteronomic law regarding prophecy contained in
Deuteronomy 18:15 ff., which asserts that there would arise in
Israel a prophet 'like Moses' to whom the people must give heed.
It is argued that this refers to the existence in Israel of a prophetic
'office', which exercised a mediating function in the covenant
relationship between Yahweh and Israel, first in a more directly
political way in the amphictyony, and then in a more 'under-
ground' fashion under the monarchy by prophets.

The fuller elaboration of support for this hypothesis so far as
individual prophets are concerned then rests on a number of
form-critical and traditio-historical arguments which endeavour
to show that the speeches of these prophets still retain evidence
of their use of forms and motifs which can be traced back to a
setting in the amphictyonic cult. In particular, such claims point
to the use of stereotyped liturgical forms which are regarded as
reflecting the earlier liturgies of the covenant cult, including ordination liturgies, ceremonies of covenant renewal, and especially
solemn acts of ritual blessing or cursing for those who obey or
disobey the covenant. It would carry us too far from our present
purpose to examine in detail here each individual form-critical
argument, or the history of each particular motif, but it should not
be left unremarked that we possess only very limited literary
evidence of the use of solemn acts of blessing and cursing in
Israel's cult, and very little other material from which to recover
a detailed picture of the liturgical forms which were in use in
Israel under the monarchy or even earlier. Similarities of form

---

[7] Cf. especially G. Fohrer, 'Altes Testament—"Amphikytyonie" und
"Bund"?', *Studien zur alttestamentlichen Theologie und Geschichte
(1949–1966)* (BZAW 115), Berlin, 1969, pp. 84–119. A. D. H. Mayes
'Israel in the Pre-monarchy Period', *VT* 22 (1973), pp. 151–70.

nd content between such liturgies and prophetic utterances,
herefore, are easy to suggest, but difficult to evaluate in detail
ecause of the very limited amount of material with which we are
ompelled to work. Even more difficult and important, so far as
uestions of method are concerned, is the task of assessing, or
emonstrating, to what extent particular forms and motifs are
eculiar to one context and are not simply part of a much wider
nd widely used stock of religious ideas and forms. In order to
how dependence on, or assimilation to, a particular liturgical
ontext it is necessary to show not only that motifs or forms from
hat context are used, but that they were consciously chosen
ecause of their relationship to that context. Otherwise they may
e merely fortuitous instances of the use of a common tradition of
naterial. It is precisely within this area of the relationship of certain
orms and motifs to specific settings that the greatest uncertainties
rise and the most serious methodological questions are raised.
iome consequences of this will be noted below.

Certainly it is very difficult to establish any adequate criteria for
howing what degree of similarity or overlap in matters of form
nd content is necessary for a sufficient case to be made which
vould enable us to claim direct dependence of one usage upon
nother. In many areas of speech and literature dealing with
natters of religion and conduct we should expect similar features
o reappear, even though no conscious or direct dependence is
ikely. Yet even in this area such arguments could be weighed more
ympathetically if the case for the existence of a prophetic covenant
nediator in early Israel could be shown to be more substantial.
n reality the evidence proves to be totally inadequate, and capable
f being better interpreted in other ways.

That the Old Testament portrait of Moses as a prophet has
rrown up out of recollections of the work of a whole succession of
mphictyonic covenant mediators is far too simplified an explana-
ion of the complex development which has taken place in pro-
lucing the present historical picture of Moses. It is far from proven
hat any part at all was played by a knowledge of the task performed
y the 'law-speakers' concerned in Alt's suggestion about the role
f the minor judges in the tribal federation.[8]

Indeed, the whole hypothesis of the amphictyonic structure of

[8] For such a view in its possible relation to the origin of the Decalogue,
f. H. Graf Reventlow, *Gebot und Predigt im Dekalog*, Gütersloh, 1962,
p. 20 ff.

pre-monarchic Israel is currently under strong attack, particularl at those points where it postulates the existence of a centralized cult and cult-leadership. Our evidence regarding the life an organization of the Israelite tribes before the introduction of th monarchy falls short of indicating directly and unequivocally th existence of a prophetic covenant mediator, and whatever rol we ascribe to the historical Joshua and to the 'elaborated' portrai of him as the leader of the tribal federation, does not point to specifically prophetic figure. Similarly, the presentation in th Deuteronomic History of a kind of succession from Mose: through Joshua and Samuel to the monarchy, is not distinctivel prophetic, and is in any case a very artificial and reflective recon struction. Thus, although the Deuteronomic school seeks to lin the work of Moses quite explicitly with that of certain prophet: there is little in the historical traditions underlying this Deutero nomic point of view to support or elaborate it.[9] The only reall significant evidence that can be adduced to support the hypo thesis of a prophetic office connected with that of an amphictyoni covenant mediator is to be found in Deut. 18:15 ff. The case t all intents and purposes stands or falls with the interpretation o this passage. Before looking at this we must bear in mind that i comes from no earlier than the seventh century B.C. when Israe and Judah had had very deep experience of the activities an preaching of certain quite outstanding prophets in the eight century. We must examine then precisely what it affirms:

Yahweh your God will raise up for you from time to time,[a prophet like me from among you, from your own kin. Hin you shall listen to. (Deut. 18:15)

[9] It has become increasingly evident that the Deuteronomic move ment expressed itself in an extensive literary activity beginning with th composition of the law book found in Josiah's reign and continuing we on into the period of the exile. Thus the activity of a 'school' rather tha of a series of individual authors and redactors seems to be evident, an although there are marked stages of theological development it appea preferable to describe the entire movement as Deuteronomic, rather tha to attempt to distinguish certain stages or parts of the movement as onl Deuteronomistic.

[10] The iterative imperfect expresses a distributive sense. Whilst could indicate a continuing succession of such prophets, and thus poir to a carefully defined 'office', this is not the necessary sense, nor is likely from the general historical context of Deuteronomy.

Clearly everything hinges here on the understanding of who the prophets 'like Moses' are that the author has in mind. Such a formal presentation of the work of prophets is unique in ancient Israel, and we have no other references which are directly comparable. Early Jewish interpretation regarded the passage in an eschatological sense and took it to indicate the coming of a special prophet in the future who would be like Moses, and who would fulfil a particular task in connection with the law.[11] However, this is to view the passage from the distinctive eschatological standpoint of post-exilic Judaism, and cannot have been the intention of the original Deuteronomic authors. This leaves us with the varied possibilities that either the law is recalling a prophetic 'office', or institution, that once existed, or else the authors are seeking to introduce a new understanding of the work of particular prophets and are themselves responsible for giving it the form of a rather stereotyped 'office'. In either case we then face the further question whether the reference is to prophets who are otherwise quite unknown to us, or whether this is intended to shed more light on prophets about whom we do have information from the books of Samuel and Kings and from the books of the canonical prophets.

H. J. Kraus[12] sees here a surviving tradition about the institution of the covenant mediator of the tribal federation whose task, he believes, had been handed on under the monarchy to certain prophetic circles. From these circles the conception of the prophetic covenant mediator came to influence the great classical prophets, especially as regards their preaching of law. Whilst this makes legitimate sense of the passage, it cannot be regarded as supported from any other information, either about the existence of an office of covenant-mediator or about the prophetic take-over of this office. It is far more satisfactory to try to understand it in the light of prophets about whose activities we do have knowledge, such as Nathan, Ahijah, Elijah and the canonical prophets of the eighth century with whose work the Deuteronomists can hardly have been unfamiliar. What is then striking is that the explicit connection of their preaching with that of Moses is not directly accounted for by the words or actions recorded of them, but must be a construction placed upon these by the Deuteronomists. Thus the most satisfactory interpretation of Deuteronomy 18:15 is that

[11] Cf. H. M. Teeple, *The Mosaic Eschatological Prophet* (JBL Monograph Series 10), Philadelphia, 1957.

[12] H. J. Kraus, op. cit., pp. 14 ff.

it represents a Deuteronomic interpretation of the work of certain prophets in Israel, rather than a historical recollection or reinterpretation of an office of covenant-mediator which had existed before the monarchy. It is not, therefore, an attempt to restore an old institution, but a reflective interpretation of the significance of the appearance of certain prophets in Israel. It seeks to comprehend the work of certain prophets, whose preaching was highly regarded in relation to the law that had once and for all been given through Moses. In this way it introduces a distinctive understanding of the role of these prophets in the light of the message that they had proclaimed. The further implications of this for the development within Israel of a clearly defined and theologically distinctive conception of the work and ministry of the prophets will be considered further in a following chapter. For our present purpose it is sufficient to note that this passage can only be made to support the hypothesis that there was a distinctive 'office' of the prophet within Israel, deriving from the old position of the covenant-mediator of the amphictyony by a very conjectural and unlikely interpretation. Whilst the passage could be explained in this way it is far from being the only, or even the most probable, explanation. Since there is no independent historical evidence that such a prophetic office once belonged to the tribal federation, we must set aside the attempt to reconstruct one as unsatisfactory. We cannot fit the work of the canonical prophets into the context of the covenant traditions of Israel by resorting to the hypothesis that they consciously regarded themselves as continuing the office of covenant-mediator, which had once belonged to the tribal federation. Whether such a covenant-mediator ever existed, and what precisely his functions may have been, is far from being clearly attested in the Old Testament. Our present concern, however, is not to re-examine the complex question of the possible institutions of the Israelite tribal federation, but simply to affirm that we do not possess any adequately clear picture of such institutions which could enable us to identify the work of the great prophets with any one of them. We cannot on this basis fit the prophets into a tradition of Israel's covenant with Yahweh.

The second of the major hypotheses regarding the role of the prophets within Israel's life as the covenant people of Yahweh concerns the claim that this covenant was formulated in accordance with the pattern of ancient Near Eastern treaty documents as a suzerainty covenant. Yahweh, on this view, was regarded as

he divine suzerain of Israel, which was bound to him in a relation-
hip akin to that of a vassal to an imperial overlord. Although this
s a hypothesis based primarily upon the form of Old Testament
ccounts of Israel's covenant with Yahweh, and the comparison
f this form with Hittite and Assyrian treaty documents, the
rguments have tended to proceed far beyond considerations of
orm. Thus matters of content and vocabulary in the prophetic
iterature have been drawn into the discussion, and a major
endency has been to interpret the prophets against a whole world
f thought which is believed to have been derived from the analogy
f Yahweh as suzerain and Israel as his vassal people. In part,
ome of the arguments relating to the hypothesis of the relation-
hip of the prophets to the amphictyonic covenant mediator have
lso been used in the discussion here, and the two interpretations
ave not necessarily been regarded as mutually exclusive.

The hypothesis necessarily starts from the acceptance that the
laims of G. E. Mendenhall, D. R. Hillers, K. Baltzer[13] and others
egarding Israel's employment of a form of covenant derived
ltimately from that of political vassal treaties is substantially
orrect. It also normally bases itself upon the belief that such a
ovenant form goes back to the age of Moses, or at least to the
re-monarchic age. Considerable modification becomes necessary
f it is argued that such a treaty form only became current in
srael much later, with the age of Deuteronomy in the seventh
entury B.C., as D. J. McCarthy has argued.[14]

On the basis of this hypothesis about the form of Israel's
ovenant with Yahweh the most significant area where comparison
s possible between material in political treaty documents and the
Old Testament prophetic literature lies in the curses of the
reaties and the threats enunciated by the prophets against Israel.
A very prominent part of suzerainty treaty documents lies in the
ong lists of curses invoked by the suzerain against his vassal if
he latter should fail to adhere to the terms of the covenant. Since
he pre-exilic prophets accuse Israel of having broken their
bligations of loyalty to Yahweh, and of having failed to maintain
he standards of law and justice which he has set them, this
epresents on Israel's part a breach of its covenant with Yahweh.
The curses which are thought to belong to the historical tradition

[13] See the works listed in note 1, page 8, and note 4, page 9.
[14] D. J. McCarthy, *Treaty and Covenant* (Analecta Biblica 21), Rome,
963.

of this covenant are then regarded as operative against Israel
What the prophets threaten as Yahweh's punishment in the way o
famine, disease, and, most of all, military defeat, are interpreted
as the application of this covenant curse to the particular historica
situations in which the prophets preached. The covenant has been
broken, and so Israel has brought down the contents of the curse
upon itself. This thesis has been worked out with a number o
examples by F. C. Fensham[15] and D. R. Hillers,[16] in detailed
comparisons of the treaty curses with the threats contained in the
prophets. Since a measure of similarity can be shown to exis
between the treaty curses and the prophetic threats, the conclusion
has been drawn that the prophets were therefore consciously aware
of this particular form of the covenant tradition in Israel, and
regarded themselves as divinely appointed to serve as its spokes
men. The theory is gravely weakened, however, once it is realized
how wide the area is from which the curses of the treaty document
have been drawn. They represent not a unique and distinctive
tradition, but are simply representative of a vast convention o
curses and cursing in the ancient Near East. Hillers fully admit
this, and has therefore only ventured his views with caution.[1]
What we lack is any evidence which can demonstrate that the
woes threatened by the prophets have been drawn directly from a
specific tradition of covenant curses, and not more generally from
a knowledge of the ills and misfortunes of life in the ancient world
which also find illustration in the curses of the treaties as well a
more generally in curse formulae. This whole attempt to define a
particular range of covenant curses, whether in the cult or in
treaty documents, has been strongly opposed by W. Schottroff[1]

[15] F. C. Fensham, 'Common Trends in Curses of the Near Eastern
and Kudurru-Inscriptions compared with Maledictions of Amos and
Isaiah', *ZAW* 75 (1963), 155–75; 'Maledictions and Benedictions in
Ancient Near-Eastern Vassal Treaties and the Old Testament', *ZAW* 74
(1962), pp. 1–19.

[16] D. R. Hillers, *Treaty-Curses and the Old Testament Prophets*
(Biblica et Orientalia 16), Rome, 1964. Cf. also his book *Covenant. The
History of a Biblical Idea*, pp. 120 ff.

[17] Hillers, *Treaty-Curses*, pp. 86–8. Cf. his remark, 'Thus what we
have called "treaty-curses" are for the most part simply traditional
maledictions which happen to occur in treaties' (pp. 86–7). Nevertheless
Hillers does assert that 'the prophets did use treaty-curses (covenant-
curses) as a basis for some of their doom-oracles' (p. 85).

[18] W. Schottroff, *Das altisraelitische Fluchspruch* (WMANT 30)
Neukirchen, 1969, *passim*.

on the grounds that the curses which we find in such contexts are simply representative of a much older convention of curses which we can trace back to Semitic life within a clan context. The basic position of Schottroff in arguing that there is nothing distinctively covenantal about the appearance of curse material in different contexts must certainly be upheld. The material is too broadly based and lacks too many explicit covenant themes for such a thesis to be tenable. We cannot therefore explain the threats of the prophets against a background of treaty curses.

In another direction the ancient Near Eastern treaty documents have been called in to provide a form-critical understanding of certain aspects of the Old Testament prophets. This is in the analysis of the form of the covenant lawsuit which appears in Isaiah 1:2-3, 10-20; Micah 6:1-5(8), and also elsewhere in the Old Testament, most notably in Deuteronomy 32, and the attempt to find its place of origin in a distinctive covenant ceremony in the cultus. G. Ernest Wright,[19] H. B. Huffmon[20] and J. Harvey[21] have all sought to identify a distinctive covenant lawsuit form, and to relate it both to the existence of a cultic ceremony of covenant renewal in ancient Israel, and also to the suzerainty treaty form.[22] Huffmon and Harvey especially concern themselves with passages in the prophets which are regarded as showing this covenant lawsuit form, but Wright, who deals primarily with Deuteronomy 32:1-25, argues that the emergence of the form in Israel is to be traced to a prophetic reshaping of the Mosaic covenant tradition. He believes that this most probably took place sometime in the second half of the ninth century B.C. in the Northern Kingdom of Israel. The fruits of this reshaping of the tradition are to be seen in the canonical prophets and in the book of Deuteronomy. Wright analyses the form of the covenant lawsuit into the following elements:[23]

[19] G. Ernest Wright, 'The Lawsuit of God. A Form-Critical Study of Deuteronomy 32', *Israel's Prophetic Heritage* (*J. Muilenburg Festschrift*), ed. B. W. Anderson and W. Harrelson, London, 1962, pp. 26-67.

[20] H. B. Huffmon, 'The Covenant Lawsuit in the Prophets', *JBL* 78 (1959), pp. 285-95.

[21] J. Harvey, 'Le RÎB-Pattern, requisitoire prophétique sur la rupture de l'alliance', *Biblica* 43 (1962), pp. 172-96. But cf. now his modified position in *Le plaidoyer prophétique contre Israel après la rupture de l'alliance. Étude d'une formule littérataire de l'Ancien Testament* (Studia 22), Paris-Montreal, 1967.

[22] G. E. Wright, op. cit., p. 52.

[23] Ibid., op. cit., pp. 52-4.

1. A call to witnesses to listen to the proceedings.
2. A statement of the case at issue by the divine judge.
3. An account of the benevolent acts of the divine suzerain.
4. The indictment.
5. The sentence.

It will be seen that this is basically a legal interpretation of the relationship existing between Yahweh and Israel in which the imagery of the law court is used to reinforce the accusations against Israel of disloyalty to Yahweh. Wright argues that, whilst it is ultimately to be derived from the form of secular treaty documents, it has been mediated through the embodiment of that form into a cultic ceremony of covenant renewal in Israel's worship. In his original essay J. Harvey[24] follows a fairly similar approach, but in his later book[25] develops this in a much more detailed and distinctive way. He sets out a detailed and comprehensive analysis of all the relevant material in the Old Testament, and comes to a very different conclusion about the origin of its form from that proposed by Wright. He accepts that this material shows the presence in Israel of a distinctive lawsuit form in which Yahweh is the accuser and Israel the accused, and that this is ultimately to be related to the form and ideology of political suzerainty treaties, but not through the mediation of a cultic ceremony of covenant renewal in which the lawsuit theme was overtly, and perhaps even dramatically, expressed. He argues that the primary origin of the form is to be found in the letters of accusation by which a suzerain declared that a vassal had broken his treaty agreement, and thereby had forfeited the privileges granted to him under the treaty and must expect to be punished. Such letters thereby represented an ultimatum and were tantamount to a declaration of war by the suzerain unless the vassal could provide an answer to the charges brought against him. Thus whilst the vocabulary and motifs are generally similar to those of the treaties themselves, the form is rather that of the letter of ultimatum by which the suzerain declared that the treaty which he had made with his vassal had been broken by the latter, and therefore the threats, expressed in the treaty in the form of curses, would be brought against him. Thus, although Harvey's view argues for a more directly literary mediation of the form from that

[24] J. Harvey, *Biblica* 43, pp. 172 ff.
[25] J. Harvey, *Le plaidoyer prophétique, passim.*

of certain categories of imperial correspondence, it, too, like the views of Hillers, Fensham, and Wright, accepts that there is a connection between the curses of suzerainty treaties and the threats expressed against Israel and Judah by the prophets. In Harvey's view, however, this is backed up by a more comprehensive framework of legal ideas and vocabulary in which the prophets show their dependence on the usages of political treaties.

First of all we should note that it is not new to suggest a connection between ancient curses and prophetic threats, since S. Mowinckel argued that the form of the prophetic woe-oracles is probably to be derived from earlier curse formulations.[26] This connection is by no means certain, but it is plausible enough. What is new in the argument connecting the prophetic threats specifically with treaty curses is the belief that the use of the treaty form, as an expression of Israel's relationship to Yahweh, constitutes an essential presupposition of the prophetic preaching, and thereby links it to a concept of covenant. Yet it is precisely this point that is not demonstrated by the analysis of the prophetic threats. Whilst there are some points of similarity to treaty curses, which are not negligible, what is strikingly absent is any indication either in form or content that the prophets have drawn directly upon a known tradition of treaty-curses. The similarities are no more than may be expected in a situation where the general conditions of life, the possibilities of misfortune, and especially the nature and methods of warfare, were very similar throughout a large area. The similarity of the prophetic threats with treaty curses is explicable simply on the recognition that descriptions of evil and misfortune were bound to show a considerable degree of similarity because all peoples were subject to essentially similar threats to life and security. There is nothing of a specifically covenantal, or treaty, character about this.

The situation is similar in regard to the 'covenant lawsuit', as it has been termed. Given the tradition of a special relationship between Israel and Yahweh, whether formulated as a covenant, or in some other way, the particular indictments of Israel which are made by the prophets and others, simply represent the application of vocabulary and imagery drawn from the processes of law to this special situation. The material is capable of being explained quite satisfactorily in this way, as E. von Waldow[27] has

[26] S. Mowinckel, *Psalmenstudien* V, rep. 1962, pp. 2, 119 f.
[27] E. von Waldow, *Der traditionsgeschichtliche Hintergrund der prophetischen Gerichtsreden* (BZAW 85), Berlin, 1963, esp. pp. 20 ff.

shown, and there is no necessity to introduce the form and contents of the treaty-curses as a necessary mediating source for it. That the prophets should have adopted the dramatic imagery of the lawsuit to reinforce their accusations against Israel is entirely conceivable, and is itself fully adequate to explain the distinctive character of the passages concerned. In a similar way the author of the book of Job has portrayed dramatically Job's sufferings and complaints as a lawsuit with God (Job 9:2 ff.; 13:3 ff., etc.), and there is no reason for supposing that any special treaty background lies behind this. This must surely be the explanation of the presence of this lawsuit form in the prophets. We do not need to call upon the existence of the treaty form in Israel, nor on borrowings from the form and content of imperial letters accusing vassals of having broken their treaty obligations, in order to explain the prophetic portrayal of a lawsuit between Yahweh and Israel. Neither, in fact, is there any need to reconstruct the pattern of a special cultic 'covenant lawsuit', since the material that is claimed to show this simply shows the adoption into cultic poetry of widely used legal imagery. That legal vocabulary and imagery, as well as traditions of covenant-making, should have found their way into Israel's cultic poetry is entirely understandable, as is evidenced by Psalm 50. Nevertheless, we are not thereby committed to recognizing a distinctive annual 'covenant review' of Israel's behaviour in the way that the presence of lawsuit imagery has been held to support. Such ideas naturally had their place among others in Israel's cultic life, especially in its Autumn Festival. In this, as in the attempt to derive the prophetic threats from the treaty curses, we must insist that the material, both in its form and content, is perfectly explicable without such a hypothesis.

This conclusion seems also to be relevant when we come to consider some of the fundamental concepts which have been held to derive from the suzerainty treaty documents. That Israel's demand for 'love' of Yahweh, or its claim to 'know' Yahweh,[28] or its idea of the Day of the Lord,[29] should require resort to political treaty documents for their explanation seems to indicate

[28] Cf. W. L. Moran, 'The Ancient Near Eastern Background of the Love of God in Deuteronomy', *CBQ* 25 (1963), pp.77–87; D. J. McCarthy, 'Notes on the Love of God in Deuteronomy and the Father-Son Relationship between Yahweh and Israel', *CBQ* 27 (1965), pp. 144–7.

[29] Cf. F. C. Fensham, 'A Possible Origin of the Concept of the Day of the Lord', *Proceedings of the Ninth Meeting of Die Ou-Testamentiese Werkgemeenschap in Suid-Afrika*, 1966, pp. 90–7.

a remarkable unwillingness to appreciate the creative possibilities of Israel's own religious life and experiences. We simply do not need to turn to such treaties to explain these basic religious concepts, which are intelligible enough in the context of Israel's own religious history and life.

In a general analysis it is clear that the attempt to interpret the role of the prophets as that of spokesmen of the covenant on the basis of contacts and similarities between the prophetic literature and ideas and forms contained in political suzerainty treaties, rests basically on the claim that this treaty form and ideology has been shown independently to have exercised a fundamental influence on Israel from the days of Moses. It is outside the scope of the present study to deal in detail with this issue, but I would wish to express my own complete lack of conviction that this has been shown, or can be shown, to have been the case. If the view were upheld that that treaty form had influenced Israel, but only at a late period with the book of Deuteronomy from the seventh century onwards, the arguments that have been discussed above would be set in a very different light, but the basic conclusions would in no way be altered. The case for arguing for such a relatively late borrowing of the treaty form and ideology in Israel is more acceptable than that which wishes to trace it back much earlier, since the Deuteronomic literature does reveal a marked and dramatic introduction of covenant vocabulary and a certain familiarity with a number of practices associated with the making of treaties. Yet even this hypothesis must be viewed with caution, and, whilst such a borrowing into the religious sphere in the seventh century B.C., of practices and ideas current in the contemporary political order, is reasonable enough, it is not the only explanation possible of the sudden flowering of covenant ideology in Israel. In particular there is a grave danger among certain scholars of regarding such political treaty documents as expressive of a kind of norm, or basic pattern of covenant-making by which all covenants are to be judged. We undoubtedly have reliable evidence of other early types of covenants and agreements in the Old Testament and elsewhere in the ancient Near East, sufficient to suggest that the so-called Suzerainty Treaties represent a highly sophisticated and distinctive development of covenant-making especially adapted to the international political scene. Old Testament ideas and forms of covenant are far from being clearly of this parentage.

If the main features of classical prophecy in Israel had already been established by the latter half of the eighth century B.C. there is no need to regard any one particular covenant form or institution as a controlling presupposition of such prophecy in Israel. Rather the reverse is more likely to have been the case, and the use of such a distinctive treaty form may have become attractive to the Deuteronomic circle in Israel because of the sharp denunciations and threats voiced by the eighth-century prophets, which had acquired a fearful realization in the downfall of the Northern Kingdom, culminating in the fall of Samaria in 721 B.C. That the development of the Deuteronomic movement in Israel, with its covenant theology was indebted to the eighth-century prophets has long been accepted by scholars, but this signifies a different connection between the prophets and the covenant from that which proponents of hypotheses about the prophetic covenant 'office' or the Suzerainty Treaty form have generally advocated.

In the light of the criticisms we have considered it does not appear possible, on the basis of form-critical and traditio-historical arguments, to formulate a presentation of the preaching of the classical prophets of the Old Testament which fits their activity into an 'office' of the covenant, such as Deuteronomy 18:15 ff. has been held to indicate. Nor can we reconstruct a covenant pattern, or ideology, drawn basically from ancient Near Eastern vassal treaties, and make this a fundamental presupposition of the prophetic preaching. Even apart from the great doubt which attaches to the claim that such a Near Eastern treaty form exercised a profound influence on Israel's understanding of its relationship to Yahweh at an early period, the features which have been held to indicate a familiarity of the prophets with the contents of these treaties, or more probably with Israelite traditions which were ultimately borrowed from such treaties, neither require nor support such a conclusion. This does not mean that the prophets as a whole had no direct concern with Israel's conception of a divine covenant, either in connection with the dynastic promise to David or with the interpretation of the Sinai revelation as a covenant. References of this nature are certainly to be found in the prophets Jeremiah and Ezekiel, although largely in secondary passages, but nevertheless these must all be examined in their own context. For a clear understanding of what such covenant traditions may have meant to the prophets we must adhere to those passages where explicit reference is made to such covenant traditions. In this regard I should now wish to modify the tendency in my earlier study, *Prophecy and Covenant*, to bring together a considerable variety of Israel's religious traditions into a relatively uniform covenant theology. This is not because indications of such a covenant theology are altogether lacking in the prophets, and in the Old Testament generally, but because it appears that the development in Israel was towards the gradual emergence of such an all-embracing covenant theology, especially in the Deuteronomic movement, and not from its acceptance as a given datum of tradition. Thus we cannot reconstruct a consistent covenant theology as a distinctive and coherent tradition underlying the preaching of the prophets, but we can see that the traditions which the prophets inherited and used had a place in the emergence of a distinctive covenant ideology in Israel. Central to this covenant ideology is the book of Deuteronomy and the Deuteronomic movement generally. What bearing this connection between the prophets and the Deuteronomic covenant theology may have upon the complex question of who the authors of Deuteronomy and the other Deuteronomic literature were cannot be dealt with here. Suffice it to mention that it is increasingly difficult in the light of the evidence to associate Deuteronomy with any one ministry of Israel's religion, either prophetic, priestly, or that of a circle of the wise. Aspects of the ideas, outlook, and speech-forms appropriate to all three areas appear to be present, suggesting that the Deuteronomic movement may have drawn elements from all three.

3

Tradition and the Prophetic Consciousness

The application of form-critical and traditio-historical studies to the prophetic literature has necessarily drawn fresh attention to those features of the prophets' preaching which they inherited and did not originate. We have noted this already in the attempts to reconstruct a picture of the prophetic 'office' which is claimed to have belonged to the early religious organization of Israel as a federation of tribes, and which several of the canonical prophets are claimed to have filled. In this way the more spontaneous and unique elements of each prophet's preaching are interpreted in a considerable measure of subordination to the derived and common elements which belonged to the historic 'office' of the prophet. The criticisms which were raised in the preceding chapter in regard to the reconstruction of this hypothetical 'office' may be sufficient to set aside the more far-reaching implications that such a view would have for the whole conception of revelation through prophetic persons in the Old Testament.

Nevertheless, it is not only in regard to the reconstruction of such a prophetic 'office' that important questions are raised about the nature of prophetic inspiration and the sources of the prophets' knowledge of the divine will. The use made by prophets of certain traditional forms of speech, and the presence of particular common ideas and motifs in their preaching raises issues relating to the essential nature of prophetic inspiration and revelation. The inter-relationship of these issues cannot be disputed. It is in the very nature of form criticism and tradition-history to examine common and repeated features which are not exclusive to one context, yet it is conversely unquestionable that the usual understanding of inspiration and revelation implies more than the simple repetition of inherited ideas and themes clothed in familiar speech-forms. It is of the very essence of prophetic revelation, as usually understood, that its messages are unique and are not merely inherited ideas and assertions. To interpret as most significant those features of the prophets which they have drawn from earlier traditions is certainly to see them in a light other than that in which they themselves would apparently have wished to be seen. Thus it is not surprising that G. Fohrer has interposed objections to an over-enthusiastic concern with the role of tradition in the prophets, not because the presence of such traditional elements is to be denied, but because the prophets can be seen to have refashioned these traditions into something new.[1] More extensively, the whole question of prophetic originality in relation to the use made by the prophets of elements of earlier traditions has been raised by M. L. Henry.[2]

In reviewing this discussion it is important to recognize that its leading problems start from a general understanding of the nature of ancient Israel's religion, and of the role of the individual within it. Essentially it must be recognized that this religion, like that of the ancient Near East generally, centred upon a cultus, and the celebration of rites at a number of major festivals. Thus the fundamental requirement of participation in this religion was 'to go up to see the face of God', three times each year on the occasions of the major festivals (Exod. 34:23).[3] There can be no doubt, therefore, that the religious activity of the individual was shared with that of the community as a whole in the cultus, and that the forms and prayers of private piety were modelled on, and derived from, those of the group.[4] Two aspects of early Israelite religion necessitate a certain *caveat* being raised here against discounting

[1] G. Fohrer, 'Remarks on Modern Interpretation of the Prophets', *JBL* 80 (1961), pp. 313 ff. Cf. also his remarks in his *History of Israelite[7] Religion*, London, 1973, pp. 282–6.

[2] M. L. Henry, *Prophet und Tradition. Versuch einer Problemstellung* (BZAW 116), Berlin, 1969.

[3] Exod. 34:23. On the whole question of the place of cult in ancient Israel's religion see S. Mowinckel, *Religion and Kultus*, Göttingen, 1953, and his articles, 'Kultus, religionsgeschichtlich', *RGG*, IV, cols. 120–6, and 'Gottesdienst II. Im A.T.', *RGG*, II, cols. 1752–6. See also R. Rendtorff, 'Der Kultus im alten Israel', *Jahrbuch für Liturgik und Hymnologie* 2 (1956), pp. 1–21.

[4] Cf. H. Ringgren, *The Faith of the Psalmists*, London, 1963, pp. 20 ff.

an element of private religion altogether. First, the inheritance of patriarchal religion, with its attachment to the structure and ideals of clan society, has led some scholars to accept that this inheritance provided a strong basis for concern with individual piety and religious experience in Israel. Most notably here mention should be made of M. Buber, who appeals to such a patriarchal inheritance as a substructure of prophetic experience in his book *The Prophetic Faith*.[5] Others too have followed such a view.[6] Whilst there is an important point here that must be borne in mind in interpreting the prophets, it seems that Buber has greatly overstressed the influence of this feature of patriarchal religion, and its continuance into the era of the great prophets. As both Gunkel and Alt have shown, the earliest patriarchal narratives make clear that, even before the spread of Yahwism, the religion of the patriarchs had accommodated itself to the cultic centres of the shrines already established in the land of the Canaanites.[7] Thus, although a strong note of individualism in Israel's religion deriving from patriarchal religion remains an interesting possibility, its influence on the prophets is far from being clearly demonstrated. Only when more direct and explicit contacts between the books of the prophets and the old patriarchal religion are demonstrable can we reckon usefully with its influence.

The second aspect of Israel's religion which points to a marked interest in individual piety and religious experience is evidenced from the Psalter. Here the presence of a very large number of individual laments points to a very real personal participation of individuals in the cultus, to an awareness that Yahweh's providence governed the lives of individual Israelites, and that a divine message could be conveyed to lay private persons. We may grant that in most cases the psalm itself would not have been composed by the individual who used it, but rather represents a composition by an accomplished psalm-writer who probably belonged to the Levitical sanctuary personnel, but nonetheless its use points to a

[5] M. Buber, *The Prophetic Faith*, New York, 1949, esp. pp. 31–42, 234–5.

[6] Cf. V. Maag, 'MALKÛT JHWH', *Oxford Congress Volume* (SVT VII), Leiden, 1960, pp. 129–53; 'Sichembund und Vätergötter', *Hebräische Wortforschung. Festschrift zum 80. Geburtstag von Walter Baumgartner* (SVT XVI), Leiden, 1967, pp. 205–18.

[7] Cf. my examination of the problem in *Abraham and David. Genesis XV and its Meaning for Israelite Tradition* (SBT Second Series 3), London, 1967, pp. 26 ff.

ep belief in action by Yahweh on behalf of individuals.[8] Such a
rsonal note in the Psalter cannot satisfactorily be explained
ay, either by regarding such individual references as personifying
e community, or by ascribing the use of all such psalms to the
ng, as the people's representative, with the claim that they have
en 'democratized'. It would certainly be in line with such a
rsonal value of religion that Yahweh should be believed to
eal himself to and through individual persons, even at times
ite outside the context of the cultus.

The note of individual religious experience in ancient Israel
eives further confirmation from the prominent place given to
tain figures in the traditions of Israel's origins, notably Abraham,
ses, Joshua and Samuel. Here, in fact, we encounter a major
ficulty since analysis of the material in these traditions in respect
its age and origin, shows that we know very little about the
ual lives of such men, and that most of what is ascribed to them
lects the interests, ideals and tendencies of later epic writers.
ey have become 'umbrella figures' under whom national and
igious ideals and institutions of later ages have been made to
lter. Particularly is this so in the case of Moses, where, as recent
dies have shown, it is notoriously difficult to be at all clear
ut his actual historical role in Israel's origins, though a vast
alth of national and religious tradition from various ages has
en ascribed to him. The same is certainly true, although to a
ser extent, of the figures of Abraham, Joshua and Samuel.
is ascribing of a large range of material to a key name has
en rise to a controversy about the dispensability of the figure of
ses in Israel's history, which was voiced by K. Koch under
e title 'The Death of the Founder of a Religion'.[9] Yet, as F.
umgärtel and others have pointed out,[10] even though it is
ficult to know what we can say positively about Moses, it is even
re difficult to dispense with him altogether. All analogies from
history of religion are opposed to such a procedure, and there
ufficient testimony in the Old Testament to individual religious

Cf. S. Mowinckel, *The Psalms in Israel's Worship*, II, Oxford, 1965,
126–45, 'Traditionalism and Personality in the Psalms'.

K. Koch, 'Der Tod des Religionstifters', *KuD* 8 (1972), 100–23.

[0] F. Baumgärtel, 'Der Tod des Religionstifters', *KuD* (1963), 223–33;
also G. Fohrer, *History of Israelite Religion*, pp. 74 f. For a very
ailed and attractive reconstruction of the work of Moses cf. S. Herr-
an, 'Mose', *EvTh* 28 (1968), pp. 301–28.

experience to make us very sceptical of any such attempt to
away completely with the contribution of Moses in this radi
fashion.

When we turn to the prophets the problems are of rathe
different kind, and there is no serious question of denying t
individuality of the prophets as persons. Yet even at this point t
relationship between the individual prophet and the group
whom we owe the collection and redaction of the book of
prophecies is far from clear. Whether the word 'disciples' a
quately describes the function of these redactors is questionab
and, in the case of Jeremiah for example, the extensive inclusi
of Deuteronomic material in the book[11] is especially notewort
in view of some earlier attempts to interpret Jeremiah as the m
individualistic of the prophets.

In the prophets the question that is most at issue is the relat
significance of ideas, motifs, speech-forms and other eleme
which can be shown, or reasonably interpreted, as features dra
by the prophets from tradition and the individual religi
experience to which the prophet testifies in his claim that Yahwe
word has come to him. What relative weight should we ascribe
the prophet's own claim to have experienced God in a dir
encounter, and to the evident fact that the prophet's words
related to themes and motifs already current in the religi
In this way the question of what is new in the prophets become
part of the question of what it is that the prophets are re
saying. Put in another way the question concerns the extent
which the prophet's claim that God's word has come to him i
personal encounter must be subordinated to the fact, evident
retrospect, that this word contains many traditional motifs a
elements. How far was the prophet conscious of this 'tradition
factor in his words?

Even though we are unlikely to be able to achieve any satisfact
overall conclusion on so broad and basic an issue, it is useful
attempt to mark out some limits within which the discussion
be continued, and to look at the nature of the prophetic literat
that we have. Here it becomes evident that attempts to appeal
directly to the prophet's experience as a means of clarifying
message have frequently led interpreters seriously astray. On
other hand it must also be said that some efforts at redressing t

[11] Cf. now especially the study of this material by E. W. Nichols
Preaching to the Exiles, Oxford, 1971.

ave so stressed the prophet's dependence on tradition as to make his the decisive feature, and the prophet merely a particular pokesman for it.

Some examples of the unsatisfactoriness of appealing to the prophet's own individual religious experience as a means of larifying his message may help to show the limitations of such an pproach. Certainly the most striking example is that of the account f Hosea's marriage in Hosea 1-3. Here the narrative accounts in Iosea 1 and 3 refer to events in the prophet's life in which he was ommanded to perform actions which have a value as signs of his nessage. The complexity of the problem of establishing precisely vhat the prophet's experience was has long been recognized, as s shown by the great variety of conclusions drawn by scholars.[12] t cannot be our more limited concern here to reconsider this ifficulty, and we must simply be content to note the wider roblem that it illustrates. The traditional view that Hosea's wife Jomer proved unfaithful, that he divorced and subsequently emarried her at God's command, and found in this a sign of God's nduring love for Israel, goes far beyond the text given. Such a iew is really the result of a methodologically unsatisfactory rocedure. It establishes a reconstruction of what the prophet's xperience is thought to have been, and then proceeds to use this) interpret the message. To understand the message itself must e our first concern, and here it becomes evident that in Hosea 1 ne message of judgement upon Israel is conveyed by all three of ne sign-names given to the children of Hosea by Gomer, and is ot primarily related to the prophet's feelings towards his wife, or to any disappointment which the prophet may have experienced over his marriage.[13] Such giving of sign-names to the prophet's hildren to convey his message is evidenced further in Isaiah,[14] nd the entire activity of the prophet in Hosea 1 must be interreted against the background of the performance of symbolic, r sign-actions by prophets as a way of giving dramatic and visible xpression to their message. Thus our primary evidence of what ne prophet's message was is contained in the children's names, ather than in the experience of his marriage. To what extent the

[12] Cf. the summary of views in H. H. Rowley, 'The Marriage of Hosea', *Ten of God*, London, 1963, pp. 66–97.

[13] Cf. especially the commentary of W. Rudolph, *Hosea* (KAT XIII, 1), p. 39 ff.

[14] Isaiah 7:3 (14?); 8:1, 3.

latter also has a sign value is less certain.[15] Similarly Hosea'
action towards the woman of Hosea 3, whether or not she i
Gomer, is primarily a sign of divine discipline and judgement, a
Hosea 3:3-4 makes plain. Hosea 3:5 must certainly be a redac
tional addition, reinterpreting the action in accordance with th
development in the direction of hope in Hosea 2, of the threatenin
names of chapter 1.[16]

In these narratives it is indisputable that the message ha
controlled and determined the account of the events, so that th
prophet's action and experience are to be understood from th
message, and not vice versa. To proceed in the reverse directio
in the case of Hosea's marriage and children has frequently le
to a failure to grasp the true nature of the message which is actuall
given. We must therefore recognize first of all the messag
character of what is recorded of the prophet's words and action
and make whatever inferences we can about his experience on th
basis of this. In consequence we cannot evaluate the truth of th
prophet's message by means of a judgement about the nature (
the experience through which it came to him. Rather we find tha
our estimate of the religious worth of the prophet's experienc
must certainly take into account the content of the messages whic
he proclaimed.

Certainly this example illustrates the danger of making an appea
to the prophet's experience, or his 'prophetic consciousness', as
basis for affirming the nature, or truth, of his message. Rather w
must see the prophet's message in relation to its own historic:
circumstances, in so far as these are known, and also in relatio
to its more immediate religious context. This certainly points t
to a concern with the traditions found, or alluded to, in th
message, which the prophets have inherited and used, eith
consciously or unconsciously. This character of the prophet
literature as 'message', even where we are presented with narr:
tives about the prophet, makes it very hard indeed to piec
together any very precise evaluation of the prophet's psychologic
experiences. This is not because 'psychologizing' is out of fashio
but because there is so little material to work on. The vario
formulae by which the prophets affirm the divine origin of the
messages are of so brief and stereotyped a kind as to provi
virtually no indication of the nature of the experiences to whic

[15] W. Rudolph, op. cit., 49 ff.
[16] W. Rudolph, op. cit., pp. 86 ff.

hey refer. Only broad categorizations into visions or auditions are
ossible, and then only of a very limited kind. The visions of
Amos, for example, contain auditive elements, and it becomes
unclear in some cases where the visionary element has ceased. This
s the case, for example in Amos 9:1, where it is not clear whether
he vision extends beyond the one verse.[17] Whatever the explana-
ion of this, it certainly does not appear that the redactors of the
ook attached any particular significance to recording and defining
he experience for its own sake.

The 'message' character of the prophetic literature, even where
t takes the form of third-person narrative accounts of events and
xperiences in which the prophet was involved is well illustrated
y the extended accounts in Jeremiah in what has frequently
een termed the 'Baruch biography' (Jer. 19:1–20:6; 26–29,
6–45, 51:59–64).[18] Here we have a series of scenes from the
rophet's ministry, some of them of a quite elaborate and lengthy
ind. Leaving aside the complex problem of authorship, and the
question of what part may have been played by Baruch in their
ollection and redaction,[19] it is immediately apparent that we in
o sense have here a 'biography'. The various scenes are chosen
or their connection with the prophet's message, and the narratives
re a means of expressing this message. Thus these accounts can
etter be described as the history of Yahweh's word by the mouth
f Jeremiah. The conflict with Hananiah, the 'false' prophet,
ntirely centres upon the question of the truth of God's word
Jer. 27–8). At no point is any detailed appeal made to the prophet's
xperience as a yardstick by which the truth of prophecy is to be
ested. Rather, of the false prophets who say to Zedekiah, 'You
hall not serve the king of Babylon' (Jer. 27:14), the affirmation is
imply made 'I have not sent them, says Yahweh, but they are

[17] This paucity of explanation regarding what the prophet actually
aw and the introduction into the visions of a marked auditory element
d K. F. Cramer, *Amos. versuch einer theologischen Interpretation*
BWANT III: 15), Stuttgart, 1930, pp. 196ff, to conclude that these are
ot true visions at all, but merely the mark of redactional stylizing. Such
view seems unwarranted in the light of the general tendency to give
nly limited reference to the visual and experiential phenomena of the
rophetic visions elsewhere in prophecy.

[18] Cf. now especially G. Wanke, *Untersuchungen zur sogenannte
Baruchschrift* (BZAW 122), Berlin, 1971.

[19] G. Wanke, op. cit., *passim*, concludes that they are not a uniform
ollection of material, and have little to do with Baruch.

prophesying falsely in my name' (Jer. 27:15). Similarly o
Hananiah, after the sharp confrontation with Jeremiah in whicl
the latter prophet threatens Hananiah with death, it is stated ver
simply: 'This very year you shall die, because you have uttered
rebellion against Yahweh' (Jer. 28:16). In so far as it is experienc
which offers any test of the truth of prophecy it here takes th
macabre form of Hananiah's death. In this way the people wil
see that Jeremiah has spoken the true word of Yahweh, althoug
the death of Hananiah is undoubtedly intended as a punishmen
and not a sign. The consistent interest in these narrative chapter
of Jeremiah in the message and not the man can readily be furthe
exemplified. In the account in Jeremiah 36 of Jehoiakim's rejectio
of Jeremiah's prophecies there is no interest in the figure o
Jeremiah himself, who is almost completely hidden in the back
ground, and all attention is directed to the fate of the propheti
word. Even when considerable allusion is made to Jeremiah'
sufferings and the severe punishments imposed upon him, ther
is no evident interest in the sufferings in themselves and in th
problems of divine justice which they raise.[20] For the author of th
accounts they simply serve to show incontrovertibly the people'
rejection of the word of Yahweh through Jeremiah. The fact o
the prophet's experience of God is accepted, and not analysed
and there is a very real interest shown at some points in th
prophetic tradition in which the prophet's word appears.[21] Thu
in the question of truth and falsehood in prophecy a very rea
awareness is shown that Jeremiah stands in an earlier tradition o
prophecy: 'The prophets who preceded you and me from ancien
times prophesied war, famine and pestilence against many countrie
and great kingdoms' (Jer. 28:8). In this respect, therefore, it i
very significant that the defence of the truth of Jeremiah's pro
phetic word is upheld by an appeal to the tradition of prophecy o
woe, and not to Jeremiah's call, or his consciousness of God
Surprisingly it is the 'tradition' which is thus used to uphold th
truth of Jeremiah's prophecy, and not his special experience o
God. Such an awareness of the distinctive role of the prophet
conceived theologically rather than institutionally, is important i
the entire presentation of Jeremiah's preaching. Much of this i

[20] Cf. P. R. Ackroyd, 'Historians and Prophets' *SEÅ* 33 (1968), p. 52
[21] Cf. G. C. Macholz, 'Jeremia in der Kontinuität der Prophetie'
Probleme Biblischer Theologie (von Rad Festschrift), Neukirchen, 1971
pp. 306–34.

no doubt due to the Deuteronomic editing which some of the prophecies have undergone, and is to be connected with the wider Deuteronomic conception of the 'office' of the prophet in Israel. Certainly it is clear that the appeal to tradition did not in itself lead to false prophecy, although it no doubt could do so.[22]

A similar marked emphasis upon the prophet's words and actions as a 'message' from Yahweh is found in the book of Ezekiel. Here, although there are several indications of a much more marked element of psychological intensity, and even abnormality, in the prophet's experience, all interest is directed away from this to the fact of the coming of the message from Yahweh. Thus the visions, the ecstatic transportations, the prophet's shaking, dumbness (Ezek. 3:26, cf. 24:27; 33:22), and possible temporary paralysis (Ezek. 3:25) are all made into vehicles of the divine message.[23] Similarly, in the accounts of the many sign-actions performed by the prophet they are recounted simply in the form of Yahweh's word to him, with no further elaboration of the activity in which they were performed in the eyes of the people.[24] Most strikingly of all the prophet's shock and silence at his wife's death is entirely subsumed into the divine message of the imminent catastrophe which is to befall Jerusalem.[25] The experience itself has become almost entirely veiled behind the message which it is made to convey. Thus the fact that by the prophet's message the action of God to and through Israel has been made known leads to the declaration that by recognizing the truth of the prophet's message the people will be recognizing God. In a surprising way, therefore, the recognition formula can be modified so that instead of affirming that the people will know that Yahweh is God, the situation can be described as the people's recognition that a prophet has been in their midst (Ezek. 2:5; 33:33). This is in no sense an indication that the prophet's experience will be an imitation, or reflection, of God, such as might be conveyed in pietistic behaviour, but simply means that through the prophet's message the people will learn the truth about God's dealing with themselves.

In one area in particular, however, the note of the prophet's experience of God is brought very much more into the foreground.

---

[22] Cf. J. L. Crenshaw, *Prophetic Conflict. Its Effect upon Israelite Religion* (BZAW 124), Berlin, 1971, p. 71.
[23] Cf. W. Zimmerli, *Ezechiel*, I (BKAT XIII, 1), Neukirchen, pp. 27 f.
[24] Cf. W. Zimmerli, op. cit., pp. 43 f.
[25] Cf. W. Zimmerli, op. cit., pp. 572 f.

This is in the call-narratives, which figure prominently in the prophetic collections of Isaiah, Jeremiah and Ezekiel. Amos refers to the fact of his call in Amos 7:14, but significantly does not seek to substantiate, or elaborate, this by any account of how it took place. Attempts to reconstruct this call on the basis of the sequence of visions narrated in Amos 7–9 are at best very hypothetical, and in any case lack any account of the all-important elements of the divine summons and commission. The closest we come to a reference to this is in Amos 3:7 f. The accounts of the call experiences of Moses (Exod. 3:1–4:9), Gideon (Ju. 6:11–40) and Saul (1 Sam. 9) show a measure of similarity to the prophetic call-narratives and must be considered in relation to them. So also the narrative of the vision of Micaiah-ben-Imlah in 1 Kings 22:5–28 has close affinities with the call-narratives of Isaiah and Ezekiel. In comparing these accounts, W. Zimmerli[26] discerns two basic types of call-narrative, the first of which is found in the calls of Moses, Gideon, Saul and Jeremiah. In this the main stress is on the divine overcoming of the inadequacy and consequent reluctance on the part of the person called. This type Zimmerli traces back to the calling of charismatic leaders in early pre-monarchic Israel. The second type emphasizes the visionary seeing of God on the part of the person called, and his being summoned into the deliberations of the heavenly council. This type is found most prominently in the cases of Micaiah-ben-Imlah, Isaiah and Ezekiel, and thus appears in a more directly prophetic context. The coupling of the divine summons and commission with a vision of God is noteworthy, and with this the emphatic forewarning to the prophet that he will suffer hostility on account of his message which will be rejected by his hearers. This appears in both types of call-narrative, and so strongly in fact is this forewarning of rejection woven into the call account that it has become a basic part of it. It appears that the fact that the prophet's word encountered hostility and rejection by the people has been a factor contributing to the necessity to reaffirm by the inclusion of such a narrative the assertion that he had nonetheless been called by God. This raises the question, which almost all commentators have felt, as to how far such a forewarning of rejection belongs to the prophet's actual call experience, and how far it reflects back his subsequent experience. To this we should perhaps add that i

[26] W. Zimmerli, op. cit., pp. 16–21.

also raises the question how far it has become a traditional element of the call-narrative as a distinctive type of prophetic account.

In this regard the fact that written prophecy first emerges with Amos, whose threat of the coming destruction of Israel was decisively rejected by the religious authorities at Bethel, and in consequence also by the royal house and court (Amos 7:10–17) can scarcely be coincidental. It was the refusal to listen to such a threat, and the subsequent banishment of Amos from the Northern Kingdom, which made it necessary to find a new way of reaffirming the threat in the form of written prophecy. This would serve both as a method of informing Israel of the threat in spite of the silencing of the prophet, and also as an attestation that the message had in fact been given. When it was fulfilled the people would be compelled to recognize that a prophet had been in their midst. It is noteworthy then that Amos countered the ban on his prophesying further in Israel by a reference to his divine call to prophesy. Since Isaiah, Jeremiah and Ezekiel all encountered hostility and a widespread rejection of their threats there is every reason to accept that the reason for including an account of their separate calls by Yahweh is the same as that which also compelled Amos to reassert the fact of his call. The type of the call-narrative therefore does seem to have a special and distinctive place within written prophecy, as a kind of historical commentary on the prophet's claim: 'Thus has the Lord Yahweh said.' The type of call-narrative which included the prophet's vision of God and his entry into the divine council still further reinforced this. The vision no doubt had its own special self-authenticating power, but it is not simply the vision as a means of revelation that is so distinctive, but the fact that it incontrovertibly identifies the one who has sent the prophet. The forewarning of rejection which is included in the prophetic call accounts serves to allay the objection that if the message had truly come from God the people would have listened to it. On the contrary these narratives show that the refusal to listen to the prophet does not cast doubt on the truth of the prophet's words, but rather confirms it. It is what the prophet has been told to expect. Thus the forewarning of rejection has become a traditional and important element of the call account, which belongs to it, in a way similar to that in which the call-narratives generally belong to written prophecy. There is thus generally a marked 'traditional' element in the call-narratives, which has led to their being assimilated into certain recognizable types. At the same time this traditional element does not deny the reality of the prophet's individual experience, but can perhaps help to elucidate it. Thus in the matter of the forewarning of rejection it would seem entirely reasonable to accept that it had become constitutive of a call experience by the time of Isaiah, and may well represent an authentic part of what the prophet experienced at his call. It does not therefore need to be regarded as depending on the prophet's own subsequent experience, but simply reflects earlier prophetic experience. All the more is this likely if Isaiah was familiar with the tradition of the preaching of Amos, as R. Fey has sought to show.[27] The presence of traditional features in the accounts of how the prophets were called by God certainly need not undermine our confidence in the genuine reality of the experiences which they describe, but they preclude our regarding such narratives as records preserved simply for the sake of recounting the experience. A certain kerygmatic function is fulfilled by such narratives, and this has both influenced the way in which they have been composed, and has no doubt also affected the way in which the prophet actually experienced his call. It is now exceedingly difficult to distinguish convincingly between these two ways in which the impact of tradition has been felt. The individual experience and the tradition have become inseparably intertwined.

It is instructive to note that in the Mari correspondence dealing with messages which had been received by prophets there is evidence of a technique for attesting the good faith of the prophet. This took the form of sending a hair and a section of the fringe of a garment, along with a report of the message given by him. These very personal tokens were apparently to serve as emblems of the prophet's submission to the recipient of the letter in that he yielded his person to the addressee.[28] It provided a way of affirming the prophet's sincerity by showing that he was willing to stake his life upon the message given. Although this was clearly an authorization of quite a different kind from that supplied by the Old Testament call-narratives, it would appear to be not entirely unrelated. It affirmed the prophet's good faith, and thus attested his sincerity in believing that God had spoken to him. This is perhaps significant as an indication that at Mari the need to

[27] R. Fey, *Amos und Jesaja* (WMANT 12), Neukirchen, 1963.
[28] Cf. W. L. Moran, 'New Evidence from Mari on the History of Prophecy', *Biblica* 50 (1969), pp. 19–23.

discriminate between prophecies was already being felt, indicating that prophecy at a very early stage was conscious of 'false' messages. Indeed, it is evident that the possibility of 'false' prophecy is inherent in the nature of all prophecy.

The question of the role played by tradition in the formulation of the call-narratives of the prophets has also come into prominence in connection with the presence of a number of cultic features contained in them. This, for example, is evident in the treatment of the Isaiah call-narrative by I. Engnell, who sees the cultic elements as forming an integral part of the call experience.[29] Even more far-reaching is the interpretation of Jeremiah's call offered by H. Graf Reventlow, where he regards the account as a description of a cultic ceremony of ordination.[30]

Admittedly the presence of certain cultic motifs and allusions reflects some relationships to a liturgical tradition, but it is far from clear that this is the immediate background of the individual call, and it is certainly doubtful whether the cultic elements add up to the provision of evidence that the call-narrative is basically a transcript of an ordination ceremony. It must be objected that a divine call and a ceremony of divine ordination are not one and the same thing, although an act of ordination may naturally be regarded as presupposing such a call. Furthermore, it is a part of the function of the call-narrative to affirm the unique individual authority which the prophet possesses, which can scarcely be regarded as achieved simply by his undergoing a distinctive, but formalized, ordination ritual. The emphasis throughout the narrative of Jeremiah's call lies upon the uniquely personal character of the prophet's call and commissioning by God. It is in this direction that M. L. Henry stresses that the cultic element in the prophet's call represents only the static background against which his personal encounter with God takes place. 'The cultic is the static background from which the recognizable features of the prophetic separate off, becoming dynamically effective in the men who are called. They necessitate submission on the part of the person so mastered in an act of spontaneous overpowering, i.e. they overcome the inner opposition to the divine claim to control of his life, and the giving up of all the familiar assurances of faith which

[29] I. Engnell, *The Call of Isaiah. An Exegetical and Comparative Study* (UUÅ 1949:4), Uppsala, 1949, pp. 32 ff.

[30] Graf Reventlow, *Liturgie und prophetisches Ich bei Jeremia*, Gütersloh, 1963, pp. 24–77.

had been given to him by tradition and the cultus up to the hour of his call.'[31]

This approach, important as it is in the recognition of the interaction of cultic and more personal and individual elements in the prophetic call experiences, seems to oversimplify the situation. It is by no means clear that the cultic elements are merely static, and that what is dynamic and prophetic separate off from this. For example the account of the ritual cleansing of Isaiah's lips given in Isa. 6:6–8 is a cultic motif which is directly prophetic and dynamic in the sense that it expresses the divine action which equips the prophet for his task. If it is objected that this event is a purely inner psychological and visionary experience of the prophet, and not a true cultic act, it nevertheless remains the case that the cultic symbolism is used to convey the claim that God has uniquely equipped the prophet for his task. The cultic tradition is employed to affirm an individual experience. It is unsatisfactory therefore to employ such highly evaluative terms as 'static' and 'dynamic' as a means of distinguishing between the cultic and individual elements of the prophet's call.[32] In its own way there is a certain dynamic quality about the cultus which makes it an important and appropriate means of expressing the prophet's encounter with God.

A related objection against unsubstantiated categorizations of the prophetic call experiences is rightly raised by J. L. Crenshaw in regard to my own earlier suggestion that Amos differed from earlier prophets in the intensity of his conviction of a divine call.[33] As Crenshaw points out, this is a value judgement which cannot be tested or substantiated by any criteria that are available to us. We do not have any detailed evidence to show that some prophets did not experience divine calls, and would not have claimed to have done so, nor can we show in what ways some calls may have been felt more intensely than others. What we can notice is that Amos was compelled to refer to the fact of his call when he was commanded by Amaziah, the priest of Bethel, not to prophesy

[31] M. L. Henry, op. cit., p. 28.

[32] Cf. H. Wildberger, *Jesaja* (BKAT X), 1968, p. 238: 'The biographical and psychological evaluation, with which scholars have been so deeply concerned, has got to proceed very carefully, because the narrative is not disposed to answer the questions which scholars put to it in this regard.'

[33] Cf. my *Prophecy and Covenant*, pp. 38 f., and J. L. Crenshaw, *Prophetic Conflict*, p. 60, note.

further in Israel. Thus the need to assert his divine call arose when his message and continued ministry were opposed and rejected. We have noted above that in the call-narratives of Isaiah, Jeremiah and Ezekiel the experience of wide-scale rejection of the message by the prophet's hearers is anticipated at the moment of the call. In this, as we have noted, it is likely that the expectation of rejection had become a traditional motif within a prophetic call-narrative by the time of Isaiah. Thus its inclusion in the report of the call may be quite authentic, as a given datum of tradition which has acquired a further significance in the individual experience of the prophet. Thus we certainly cannot maintain that it is the traditional elements which are 'static', whilst what is truly prophetic and dynamic is original and new. The prophetic call-narratives show a complex interplay of traditional and new elements which makes the question of the relationship between the prophets and tradition a real one.[34] To answer such a question we should not expect to attain any simple formula, either in the contrast of static and dynamic, or cultic and prophetic. The traditional elements are not simply those motifs and allusions which derive from the cultus, nor is the tradition merely static. We may recall again that in the account of the confrontation between Jeremiah and Hananiah, which is now narrated in a form which brings out certain theological interests, the condemnation of the 'false' prophets is simply that 'Yahweh has not sent them' (Jer. 27:15; 28:9), and yet this can be further verified and elaborated by reference back to a tradition of prophetic preaching of woe (Jer. 28:8).

In conclusion, we may summarize certain points relevant to the debate about tradition and the prophetic experience of God. When an individual prophet asserted the divine origin of his message, and affirmed that he had been specially chosen and called of God to proclaim this, he was undoubtedly testifying to a particularly immediate consciousness of God. Yet at the same time, both in its form and content, this message shared a connection with earlier prophetic messages and with other areas of Israel's religious life. Not least the classical prophets appear to have been well aware that they stood in a prophetic tradition and fulfilled a particular role in the divine ministry to Israel. Their consciousness of this is shown by the way in which they presented their messages, and has certainly entered deeply into several features of what they

[34] Cf. the comments of W. Zimmerli on the account of Ezekiel's call, op. cit., p. 21.

actually said. It does not appear therefore that the prophet was deliberately abandoning all earlier religious traditions, although he certainly believed that he was adding something fresh and important to them. Further to this, those circles in Israel to whom we owe the collection and redaction of the prophets' words, and who in several cases supplemented them with narratives about the prophets, also show in their editorial activities a consciousness of tradition, both as regards the nature of the prophet's task, and also in respect of the meaning and application of his words. Frequently this meant a 'development' of the prophet's original words in order to bring out their significance for a later age, and for the further history of the institutions to which they referred. In this way the words of the great prophets themselves became a part of the tradition about certain of the major institutions of Israel, especially the temple and the kingship. The prophetic consciousness of God therefore did not mean either an abandoning of tradition, nor yet simply a wholehearted embracing of it. The prophet himself both drew upon, modified, and added to the religious traditions of Israel, at times affirming it, and at others rejecting it. No one simple approach therefore can adequately cover the prophet's relationship to tradition, and it is essential to remain open to the varied possibilities which each passage and each situation allows.

4

The Role of the Prophet according to Israelite Tradition

In a foregoing chapter we have seen the unsatisfactory nature of the attempts to relate the prophets to a particular 'office' of the covenantal order between Yahweh and Israel which existed before the introduction of the monarchy. There is no substantial evidence to show that the prophetic ministry was in any conscious way a revival, or continuation, of the earlier office of the mediator, or law-speaker, of such an amphictyony. If we also reject the hypothesis that the forms and ideology of a divine covenant, based on the pattern and ideas of suzerainty treaties, formed the unmentioned presupposition of a variety of threats and accusations made by the prophets, we cannot relate the prophets to the idea of a divine covenant in any such direct way. Had such an office existed, or such a framework of treaty ideology influenced the prophetic preaching so decisively, it is inconceivable that no explicit mention of either would have been made. In this regard we must accord full endorsement to the objections of L. Perlitt.[1] Yet in turn Perlitt dismisses the prophetic concern with the covenant too sharply, once he has shown that these theories are insupportable and that the reference to Israel's covenant with Yahweh made in Hosea 8:1 is not authentic to the prophet.[2] In this case, for example, we must ask why a redactor has introduced a reference to Yahweh's covenant and its law here, and what redactional purpose it was intended to serve. It is evident that such redactional work on the

---

[1] L. Perlitt, *Bundestheologie im Alten Testament*, pp. 129 ff.

[2] L. Perlitt, ibid., pp. 146–9. Perlitt fully affirms that Hos. 8:1 relates to the Deuteronomistic covenant theology.

eighth-century prophets is not isolated, but must certainly be related to the wider framework of similar redactional activity which is marked both in Amos and Hosea. Thus, although the word 'covenant' is not mentioned in the secondary passage Amos 2:4, this passage contains a broad indictment of Judah for forsaking Yahweh's law which is very similar to Hosea 8:1. Hence, although Hosea 8:1 is alone in Hosea in its explicit reference to Yahweh's covenant with Israel at Sinai, it is part of a redaction which is more extensive and which bears comparison with similar redactional work in the book of Amos.

Before looking at this redactional work, with its interest in covenantal ideas in more detail, we must refer back again to the striking significance of the passage in Deut. 18:15 ff., with its affirmation of the divine purpose in sending to Israel a prophet 'like Moses'. This Deuteronomic text is not, as we noted above, recalling an ancient office of the amphictyony, but it is certainly pointing to an awareness of the existence in Israel of prophets whose words and activity were being interpreted in a highly distinctive way. Not only is Moses regarded as a prophet, as in Hosea 12:13, but a very striking categorization of the preaching of the prophets is accomplished by its being set alongside that of Moses, which, as Deuteronomy 4:44 shows, was regarded as *torah*, interpreted in a very juridical and covenantal way. Thus Deuteronomy 18:15 ff. presents an interpretation of the work of certain unnamed prophets which views it as functioning within the order of the covenant which was inaugurated on Mount Horeb (Sinai) by Moses. If the prophets themselves did not consciously inherit this understanding of their 'office', as we have discussed in the preceding chapter, then it must be the Deuteronomic authors of this law who were seeking to interpret the work of certain prophets in this highly original way. The prophets, with all the freedom and range of their preaching, were being interpreted as set within certain well-defined theological limits. Admittedly, some uncertainty must remain here because we cannot define precisely which prophets it is that the law of Deuteronomy 18:15 ff. has in mind. If, as seems most probable, it is referring to such figures as Elijah, Elisha, Amos and Hosea, who are all otherwise prophets known to us from the Old Testament traditions, then it is adding a quite new and unexpected dimension to the interpretation of their preaching. Their message is claimed to possess a covenantal reference and context relating to Moses,

which their own words do not explicitly show.[3] In this way the
Deuteronomic law of the prophet provides a wider context for an
understanding of the preaching of these prophets than that
preaching originally explicitly warranted. The question of the
concern of the eighth-century prophets with the covenant,
therefore, is not concluded simply by noting their silence about the
Sinai covenant. A redactor has explicitly linked Hosea's preaching
with the Sinai covenant in Hosea 8:1, and this covenantal interest
shows contacts with the further redaction of Hosea.[4] When this is
compared with the Deuteronomic interpretation of the role of the
prophet as a divine spokesman 'like Moses', then it is reasonable
to conclude that there is some connection between this Deuteronomic understanding of the role of the prophet and at least some
of the redactional work that has been accomplished in the literary
presentation of Hosea. Furthermore it is wholly in line with
this that several scholars and most notably H. W. Wolff, have
argued strongly for a Deuteronomic redaction of the book of
Amos.[5] That a connection between the preaching of Hosea and
the origins of the Deuteronomic movement existed has long been
argued by scholars,[6] and it would be wholly in line with this that
some of the redaction of the book of Hosea should have taken
place in circles closely connected with the Deuteronomists.

It may at this point appear that there is almost a tendency
towards a 'pan-Deuteronomism' in recent scholarly assessment
of the religious developments in Israel and Judah from the eighth

---

[3] L. Perlitt, op. cit., p. 136, goes so far as to say that the message of
Amos prohibits covenant theology.

[4] Cf. Hos. 1:7; 2:5; 4:15; 5:5b, 6:11a; 8:14; 10:11. It is unlikely that
this redactional work took place all at one time, or by one hand, but it
does display a number of consistent tendencies regarding the unity of
Israel, and hence the applicability to Judah of prophetic warnings
originally delivered to the Northern Kingdom. It also sees a great importance in a future hope centring on a restoration of the nation as a single
kingdom under a Davidic ruler. Cf. esp. Hos. 2:5. It thus shows important
affinities with some of the main lines of Deuteronomic thought.

[5] Cf. H. W. Wolff, *Joel und Amos* (BKAT XIV, 2), Neukirchen, 1967,
pp. 129, 137 f. W. H. Schmidt, 'Die deuteronomistische Redaktion des
Amosbuches', *ZAW* 77 (1965), pp. 168–93. U. Kellermann, 'Der
Amosschluss als Stimme deuteronomisticher Heilshoffnung', *EvTh* 29
(1969), pp. 169–83.

[6] Cf. H. W. Wolff, *Hosea*, p. xxvi, 'Whole movements of thought,
which are important for the Deuteronomic paranesis, are found for the
first time in Hosea.'

DP

to the sixth centuries B.C. In this regard we may note that I.
Willi-Plein, in a major work on the redaction of the books of
Amos, Hosea and Micah, dissents from the ascription of much of
this material, particularly in Amos, to a Deuteronomic circle.[7]
Admittedly not all this redactional work was accomplished at a
single stroke, nor therefore probably by a single group, and overall
it represents a very extended process. Yet what is striking in its
main features is a compact range of basic assumptions: the belief
that Israel is one (cf. Amos 3:1), so that Yahweh's word to one
part can be applied to the whole; i.e. Yahweh's word to Israel
can also be applied to Judah. Further there is the assumption that
a revealed *torah* is a fundamental basis of Israel's life so that the
many detailed indictments which constitute the prophetic invective
can be summarized as forsaking the *torah* of Yahweh revealed at
Sinai (so. Amos 2:4; Hos. 8:1). Strikingly too, in contrast with
the sharp and absolute nature of the original prophetic threats,
there is a strong emphasis on the promise of Israel's ultimate
restoration as a unified people once more under a Davidic head
(Hos 2:5; Amos 9:11–15). In this way the original note of warning
is developed into a strong appeal to repentance, which remained
relevant after the catastrophes foretold by the prophets had taken
place. These ideas form a basic part of the Deuteronomic theology,
as exemplified in the Deuteronomic law, and more fully elaborated
in the Deuteronomic History. If this appears to indicate a kind
of 'pan-Deuteronomism' then it must be noted that the Deuteronomic theology does hold a quite central position in Israelite
thought.[8] This is especially true in relation to the dominant part
played by the Deuteronomic movement in creating and developing
a theology of covenant in Israel, as has recently been re-emphasized
by L. Perlitt.[9] We must also keep in mind that this fresh interest

[7] I. Willi-Plein, *Vorformen der Schriftexegese innerhalb des Alten
Testaments* (BZAW 123), Berlin, 1971, esp. pp. 60, 63–4 for a criticism
of the work of Schmidt and Wolff on Amos. Also the detailed and extensive
treatment of the redaction of Hosea (pp. 115 ff.) opposes any significant
Deuteronomic assessment of the work.

[8] Cf. S. Herrmann, 'Die konstruktive Restauration. Das Deuteronomium als Mitte biblischer Theologie', *Probleme Biblischer Theologie*
(von Rad Festschrift), pp. 155–70, Munich, 1971.

[9] L. Perlitt, op. cit., pp. 7 ff. Perlitt appears too rigid in asserting an
almost exclusively Deuteronomic interpretation of covenant in Israel
with a consequent dismissal of earlier and divergent ideas and traditions
of covenant such as are associated with the patriarchs and with the
monarchy. E. Kutsch, *Verheissung und Gesetz, passim.*, recognizes a much

in the redaction of the books of Amos and Hosea has not primarily arisen as a further attempt to find a fresh stratum of secondary material in these books, but as an attempt to identify the origin and purpose of material that scholars have long recognized to be secondary. In this respect its importance as an early form of interpretative exegesis cannot be overlooked. It is a primary guide to those religious interests in Israel and Judah which have led to the formation of a collection of prophetic literature, with a unique, and ultimately canonical, authority.[10]

This interest in the redactional work on the books of Amos and Hosea highlights a very significant change in recent approaches to the prophetic literature, which may broadly be included under the heading of redaction criticism. In this there is a renewed concern to understand and interpret the form and contents of the books as a whole, and not simply to evaluate them out of concern to recover the original preaching of the prophets. Since in no case has the extant book been given its final shape by the prophet himself whose preaching it records, a great importance attaches to an understanding of the processes by which the prophet's original spoken word was committed to a book, or collection of books. For a considerable time scholars have worked with the assumption that the circles to whom we owe the literary formulation of the preaching of the great prophets were groups of 'disciples' of the original prophet-masters. It is to these, it is believed, that we owe the careful memorizing and recording of the prophet's preaching, and the elaboration of this with narratives about the prophet's activities and experiences. Yet the prophetic literature is strangely silent about the existence of these circles of disciples, and the passage in Isaiah 8:16 which is frequently alluded to in support of their existence in the case of Isaiah, cannot, with any confidence, be said to do so.[11] In the case of Baruch, the scribe whom Jeremiah used to write down his oracles, he is not called a disciple and his role in the prophet's life is determined by his function as a scribe. Even so, however close his relationship to Jeremiah may have been, he appears in isolation and not as one of a

greater variety of meanings in the Hebrew concept of *berith*, but stresses very heavily that it originally described the unilateral action of imposing an obligation.

[10] I. Willi-Plein, op. cit., pp. 1 ff.

[11] Cf. G. Fohrer, *Introduction to the Old Testament*, London, 1970, p. 359.

group of disciples. Significantly, too, the book of Jeremiah shows some of the most marked characteristics of extensive redaction in a direction which far exceeds the role of a disciple in recording his master's words, and which certainly cannot all be ascribed to Baruch.

Throughout the prophetic literature, with the possible exception of Deutero-Isaiah, it is unlikely that the process of writing down the prophecies was accomplished by the hand of the prophet himself. Nevertheless, in view of the evident rejection of their preaching experienced by many of the prophets, we ought to consider the possibility that they took steps to secure that their messages were preserved in writing as a witness against the day when their threats would be fulfilled. This is clearly what Jeremiah did when he was faced with opposition to, and evident restriction of, his public preaching (Jer. 36). The question at issue is whether 'disciples' adequately describes the function and activity of those who have subsequently preserved the prophet's words, and who have given to them an extended literary form. It is the function of a disciple to preserve and carry forward his master's teaching, whereas what has taken place in the prophetic literature far exceeds this. In the case of Amos there is a marked tension between the prophet's original threats of Israel's downfall and the redaction which looks to the ultimate restoration of Israel. Similarly, in Hosea, the redaction of the book has introduced a marked political definition to the expressions of hope delivered by the prophet. In consequence of an unwillingness to admit the presence of this redactional dress in the book of Hosea, I. Engnell arrived at a highly unconvincing picture of the prophet as a pro-Judean, pro-Davidic, preacher of hope.[12] Furthermore there are substantial points of connection between the redaction of Amos and Hosea and the theology of the Deuteronomic movement, and this Deuteronomic element is even more marked in the book of Jeremiah. Even if we should hesitate to suppose that it is the same group who have been responsible for all this work, we cannot overlook the important similarities of outlook which exist.[13] Such

[12] Engnell, *Critical Essays on the Old Testament*, London, 1970, p. 141, especially note 43.

[13] In this regard it is interesting to recall the earlier hypothesis of S. Mowinckel regarding the extensive activity of Isaiah's disciples from the eighth to the sixth centuries B.C. Such disciples, Mowinckel believed, were deeply involved in the origin of the Decalogue and the book of Deuteronomy. Cf. S. Mowinckel, *Jesaja-Disiplene. Profetien fra Jesaja til Jeremia*, Oslo, 1926.

activity points to the work of a much wider group than can be satisfactorily described as the disciples of either one, or several, of the great prophets. We are certainly faced here with the literary deposit of a quite extensive religious activity which attached great importance to the preaching of the prophets. Those who were responsible for this literary work were also deeply interested in understanding Yahweh's relationship to Israel as a covenant, as is so marked a feature of the book of Deuteronomy. Thus they were in a special way interested in seeing the prophets against a background of the covenant of Sinai-Horeb.

This leads us to consider a further question about the relationship of the Deuteronomic movement to the preaching of the great pre-exilic prophets of Israel. In his study of the scope and composition of the Deuteronomic History, M. Noth drew fresh attention to the surprising fact that, although parts of this history make extensive reference to the activities of prophets, it passes over in almost complete silence the work of the canonical prophets, with the exception of Isaiah.[14] Even in this latter case the narratives in which Isaiah figures give only a very restricted presentation of his message in its relation to Sennacherib's invasion of 701 B.C. This is so coloured as to raise many questions of a historical and theological nature.[15] Noth explained this unexpected silence about the great prophets in the Deuteronomic History as an indication that the author did not have before him material relating to these men. Yet this is a very remarkable conclusion to be forced to draw, and one which has increasingly aroused scepticism and a call for revision. In the general lines of interpretation adopted by the Deuteronomic History the note of warning certainly bears comparison with the threats of the great prophets, and that History points to God's activity in the prophetic word as a primary mode of his intervention in history. It is clear that the authors of the History would have been interested in the prophets' preaching, and yet it appears surprising that they should have had no access to the traditions in which it was collected. This latter conclusion is quite evidently not the case in regard to Jeremiah, who was active in Jerusalem throughout the last days of Judah which form for the Deuteronomic History the climax of the whole narrative.

[14] M. Noth, *Überlieferungsgeschichtliche Studien I*, Halle 1943, p. 97 f.
[15] Cf. B. S. Childs, *Isaiah and the Assyrian Crisis* (SBT Second Series), London, 1967, pp. 20 ff.

The events of these days are described without mention of Jeremiah, even though the authors of the History drew their account in 2 Kings 25:1–26 from the 'Baruch' narrative of Jeremiah 39–41.[16] Surprisingly all reference to Jeremiah's part in these events is omitted. Furthermore Jeremiah's preaching has come down to us in a thoroughly Deuteronomic dress in which lengthy prose sermons are included which have been formulated in the style and ideology of the Deuteronomists. This has long been recognized since the work of B. Duhm and S. Mowinckel on the source materials of the book of Jeremiah, even though varying estimates are possible of the relationship which these sermons bear to Jeremiah's actual preaching. The 'Baruch' narrative material in Jeremiah also shows a close relationship to the fundamental religious ideas and aims of the Deuteronomic movement. There are, therefore, very strong indications to support the view that close contacts existed between the authors of the Deuteronomic History and the circles to whom we owe the preservation and redaction of the book of Jeremiah. The silence of the Deuteronomic History about the great prophets can then better be explained as a consequence of their preaching having been regarded as the subject of a related literary collection, which was independently available, than as an indication that the authors of the History were ignorant of it. Such a view gains added strength if it is conceded that the books of Amos, and also of Hosea to some extent, have undergone a 'Deuteronomic' redaction.

In line with this general question some interesting attempts have been made to reconsider the apparent silence of the Deuteronomic History about the great prophets. O. Eissfeldt has reawakened interest in the view, originally proposed by J. Wellhausen, that in 1 Kings 13 we have a popular, although rather garbled, version of the preaching of Amos, even though this wrongly locates Amos in the reign of Jeroboam I (922–901) and not Jeroboam II (786–746).[17] The presence of a very popularized and distorted legend about Amos, however, would not in any way strengthen the claim that the authors of the Deuteronomic History were familiar with a collection of his prophecies such as are now preserved in the book of Amos. More significant has been

[16] M. Noth, *Überlieferungsgeschichtliche Studien*, pp. 86 f., especially note 1, p. 87.

[17] O. Eissfeldt, 'Amos und Jona in volkstümlicher Überlieferung', *Kleine Schriften* IV, Tübingen, 1963, pp. 137–42.

the work of H. W. Wolff in arguing that the Deuteronomic account of Josiah's reform given in 2 Kings 22–3 saw in Josiah's destruction of the sanctuary at Bethel a fulfilment of the threat pronounced by Amos (Amos 9:1), and that a reflection of this interpretation is also to be seen in the editing of the book of Amos.[18] In a very intriguing suggestion also F. Crüsemann[19] has argued that the seemingly gratuitous comment in 2 Kings 14:27: 'But Yahweh had not said that he would blot out the name of Israel from under heaven . . .' is an indirect allusion to the preaching of Amos with its threat 'an end has come upon my people Israel' (Amos 8:2). Undoubtedly the setting of the Historian's comment in the reign of Jeroboam II makes this suggestion plausible, and it would certainly be in line with the editing of the book of Amos with its hope of Israel's restoration. In support of his argument Crüsemann argues strongly that the authors of the Deuteronomic History were familiar with traditions of the work of the great prophets. Whatever the validity of these interpretations of individual points of detail in the Deuteronomic History, it appears far more likely that the authors were aware of collections of traditions about the great prophets which they regarded as available independently than that they were ignorant of such material. Such a negative conclusion is neither necessary nor probable.

This general discussion about the familiarity of the authors of the Deuteronomic history with traditions of the work and preaching of the classical pre-exilic prophets is of very great significance for an understanding of a key passage in their work. In 2 Kings 17:13–14, where the Deuteronomic authors reflect on the reasons for the downfall of the Northern Kingdom with the fall of Samaria in 721 B.C., the role of prophets in Israel's history is singularly emphasized and interpreted:

> Yet Yahweh warned Israel and Judah by every prophet and every seer, saying, 'Turn from your evil ways and keep my commandments and my statutes, in accordance with all the law which I commanded your fathers, and which I sent to you

[18] H. W. Wolff, 'Das Ende des Heiligtums in Bethel', *Archäologie und Altes Testament* (Festschrift K. Galling), Tübingen, 1970, pp. 287–98; *Joel und Amos*, pp. 135–8.

[19] F. Crüsemann, 'Kritik an Amos im deuteronomistischen Geschichtswerk. Erwägungen zu 2 Könige 14, 27', *Probleme Biblischer Theologie* (G. von Rad Festschrift), Neukirchen, 1971, pp. 57–63.

by my servants the prophets.' But they would not listen, but
were stubborn as their fathers had been, who did not believe in
Yahweh their God. (2 Kings 17:13-14)

This asserts that it was the function of the prophets, who are
regarded as a recognizable group, to warn both Israel and Judah
to repent and to keep the law (*torah*), which had itself been given
to the people by prophets. Thus the prophets are presented as
preachers of repentance whose message was a call to return to the
law. In line with the entire History this can only refer to the
Mosaic law given at Sinai-Horeb. Thus, like the law of Deuteronomy 18:15ff. the prophets are regarded as preachers of the law
'like Moses', so that they are seen as ministers of the covenant.

This is certainly a highly distinctive characterization of the
prophetic preaching, which must be seen in the light of the
other Deuteronomic interpretations of prophecy which we have
already considered. Once again it raises the problem of the identification of the prophets concerned. O. H. Steck, in a study of the
passage and its presuppositions,[20] seeks to explain its background
in line with H. W. Wolff's suggestions about the spiritual background of Hosea.[21] He suggests that the Levitical circles who stood
behind Deuteronomy had come to be associated in the Northern
Kingdom with prophetic circles who were loyal to Yahweh. This
association took place either in Hosea's time or sometime after-
wards. As a result of this connection, which gained support from
the fact that both groups traced their traditions back to Moses,
the content of the prophetic message came to be characterized as
torah, in a way that onesidedly stressed the Levitical concern with
torah.

Yet this hypothesis is scarcely necessary as an explanation of the
distinctive character of the statement about the role of the prophets
in the Deuteronomic History. Its purport is sufficiently in line
with other aspects of the Deuteronomic interpretation of prophecy
to lead us to conclude that it represents a quite marked feature of

[20] O. H. Steck, *Israel und das gewaltsame Geschick der Propheten.
Untersuchungen zur Überlieferung des deuteronomistischen Geschichtsbildes
im Altes Testament, Spätjudentum und Urchristentum* (WMANT 23),
Neukirchen, 1967, esp. Excursus III: Die Entstehung der generellen
Dtr. Prophetenaussage und des Moments des gewaltsamen Geschicks,
pp. 199-201.

[21] H. W. Wolff, 'Hoseas geistige Heimat', *Ges. Stud. zum A.T.*
(ThB 22), Munich, 1964, pp. 232-50.

the Deuteronomic theology generally, and is an attempt to interpret the role of the prophets as falling within the divine covenant of Horeb. Thus the Deuteronomic covenant theology is here being impressed on the prophets, who are almost certainly to be regarded as the same prophets who were in mind in Deuteronomy 18:15 ff. Thus these are the great figures like Elijah and Elisha, and were no doubt intended to include among their number the eighth-century figures of Amos and Hosea, who prophesied against Israel, and perhaps also Isaiah and Micah among those who prophesied against Judah. Such a view would, of course, be greatly strengthened if the case for a general familiarity with traditions about these prophets on the part of the authors of the Deuteronomic History is conceded.

Interestingly enough the interpretation of the role of the prophets in 2 Kings 17:13 ff. continues with a reference to Israel's rejection of this prophetic call to repentance, which as O. H. Steck shows, is later developed into a picture of the prophet as a martyr figure.[22] This consciousness of rejection is, as we have noted, a marked feature of the understanding of the prophet's role in the call-narratives of Isaiah, Jeremiah, and Ezekiel. It is also reflected in Amos 2:10–12, where Amos, or his Deuteronomic redactor as H. W. Wolff believes,[23] points back to Israel's rejection of the preaching of the prophets. We may cite with relevance Wolff's own conclusions regarding the prophets who are being referred to here: 'By the prophets the Deuteronomic preacher has in mind the series of authoritative spokesmen from Moses onwards (Deut. 18:15, 18), through Elijah, Micaiah-ben-Imla etc., right up to Amos himself and beyond him (cf. Amos 2:12b with 7:16b).'[24]

There is good reason for believing therefore that the Deuteronomic interpretation of prophecy contained in 2 Kings 17:13 ff. is related to that given in Deut. 18:15 ff., and represents a significant Deuteronomic interpretation of the work of the great prophets as a role instituted by Yahweh to be a ministry of the covenant inaugurated by Moses. Thus it sets this preaching within a theological context of covenant ideas and vocabulary which it did not previously possess, and interprets it quite distinctively as

[22] O. H. Steck, op. cit., pp. 60 ff.
[23] H. W. Wolff, *Joel und Amos*, pp. 137 f., 172, 205 ff. For Amos 2:10, cf. Deut. 29:4 and also Deut. 8:2.
[24] H. W. Wolff, *Joel und Amos*, p. 207.

torah, which is to be set alongside the *torah* of Moses. It i
summarized as a call to Israel to return to this *torah*. In this wa
the characteristic connection between the prophetic threats an
particular historical situations and events is broadened into
much wider appeal, which is set at a certain remove from th
particularity of individual events. The warning of impendin
disaster passes, but the need to repent endures.

It is clear from this examination of the development withi
Israel of a Deuteronomic tradition about the work and destin
of the prophets that there had emerged by the middle of the sixtl
century B.C. an overall interpretative assessment of their message
The laws regarding prophecy in Deuteronomy and the assertion
of the Deuteronomic Historian provide the earliest stage to whicl
we can penetrate back to obtain any kind of external witness t
the religious interests which led to the preservation of the prophetic literature. For the rest we are dependent upon the interna
evidence of the prophetic writings themselves, with the indication
they provide of redaction and interpretation. Nevertheless, limite
as it is, this evidence of the Deuteronomic interpretation of th
role of the prophets, is wide-ranging in its implications. Not leas
it provides us with a very important key to understanding ho
there grew up in Israel a conception of 'true' prophecy whicl
could be contrasted with the activities of rival 'false' prophets
The laws of Deuteronomy regarding prophecy have primaril
been formulated with this problem in mind. The true prophet i
a prophet 'like Moses', and his words are those that the peopl
must heed.

The difficulties felt by modern scholars in reconstructing an
clear principle by which to distinguish the 'true' from the 'false
prophet are well evidenced by the variety of solutions proposed
Neither of the general schemes of doom/salvation or cult prophet
free prophet can satisfactorily provide a basis on which to dif-
ferentiate the true prophet from the false. It is clear that at leas
Hosea and Isaiah among the classical prophets of pre-exilic Israe
included assurances of future restoration and blessing in thei
preaching, and it is arguable that we have preserved among th
canonical prophets the utterances of those who were cult-
prophets.[25] Even if this is contested we have no clear grounds fo

[25] Cf. the thesis of Jörg Jeremias, *Kultprophetie und Geschichtswerk
ündigung in der späten Königszeit Israels* (WMANT 35), Neukirchen
1970, who argues that both Nahum and Habakkuk were cult prophet

supposing that at any point Israel ever regarded formal attachment to the cult as a criterion for determining the falseness of a prophet's preaching. If it had been so we should expect to find some evidence of it in the Deuteronomic laws regarding false prophets. If we abandon these over-simple schemes we may fall back on the broader contention that false prophecy is that which proved itself to be so by its non-fulfilment (cf. Deut. 18:21f.). This also, however, is unsatisfactory because it is unable to account for the presence of 'unfulfilled' prophecies in the canonical prophets which were nevertheless preserved. We have, for example, Micah's prediction in the eighth century B.C. of the fall of Jerusalem, which appears to conflict with the prophecies of his contemporary Isaiah that the city would be protected by God. That the prophecy was regarded as unfulfilled, even as late as Jeremiah's time, is shown by Jeremiah 26:17–19, even though Micah's prophecies were undoubtedly preserved.[26] Very significantly an important aspect of the redactional work on the prophetic books was to adapt and reinterpret prophecies in the light of later historical circumstances, particularly reinforcing promises of Israel's restoration alongside the starkness of the prophetic threats. This certainly indicates that the question of the 'truth' of prophecy was seen to be a larger truth than could be contained within a simple prediction-fulfilment formula. Thus, for example, if Wolff has correctly interpreted the character of the Deuteronomic editing of the book of Amos, this interpreted the threat uttered by Amos against the sanctuary of Bethel far beyond the historical situation pertaining in the prophet's own days, and set it against the very different background of Josiah's reform. Certainly it appears quite inadequate, from the point of view of the contents and redaction of the prophetic literature, to assert the truth or falsehood of prophecy simply on the basis of a single historical fulfilment of the prophetic word.[27]

If, then, we cannot fall back on any one single formula for

who proclaimed judgement against Israelites, but not against Israel as a whole. Thus, although these cult prophets were not simply prophets of assurance, their threats of doom did not have the same range as those of the free, unattached prophets.

[26] Cf. also Ezekiel's revision of his threat of the fall of Tyre to Nebuchadnezzar (Ezek. 29:17–20 with 27:1–28:19), and the similiar phenomenon of revision of an earlier prophecy in Is. 22:24–5, where the promise of v. 20–3 is completely altered.

[27] Cf. J. L. Crenshaw, *Prophetic Conflict. Its Effect upon Israelite Religion* (BZAW 124), Berlin, 1971, pp. 49–52.

Israel's own understanding of what constituted the truth or falsehood of prophecy we must look for a solution in a different direction. This points us to a recognition that there slowly emerged
in Israel and Judah, from the eighth century onwards, a conception
of 'true' prophecy which was in principle canonical. Among
certain circles in Israel, which must have stood very close to the
Deuteronomists in their outlook, there grew up a regard for certain
prophets and their message which vested in them a kind of
canonical authority. This emergent conception of the 'true'
prophet saw him as a figure 'like Moses', and the outcome of this
conception is to be seen in Deuteronomy 18:15, 18 and 2 Kings
17:13 f.[28] For the Deuteronomic circle who stand behind these
passages certain prophets had become singled out as 'true'
spokesmen of Yahweh's word, and were to be distinguished from
the 'lying' prophets who had misled the nation. This does not
of course, imply that such a Deuteronomic conception of true
prophecy worked in an arbitrary fashion. It is evident from
Deuteronomy 18:22 that the Deuteronomists did expect the words
of the true prophet to validate themselves by their historical fulfilment, but this was lifted by the Deuteronomists from the
arbitrariness of isolated instances into the context of the larger
and continuing crisis that faced Israel and Judah during the
periods of Assyrian and Babylonian domination. The very notion
of the 'fulfilment' of the prophetic word was thereby given a
larger and more significant interpretation. We may legitimately
infer from 2 Kings 17:13-14 that there grew up in the Deuteronomic circle a broadly based conception of the truth of prophecy
which was responsible for recognizing in the message of certain
prophets a unique authority. By relating this message to the
unique authority of the *torah* of Moses, as presented by the book
of Deuteronomy, the basic groundwork of a canonically conceived
work of 'the Law and the Prophets' was established.

This Deuteronomic interpretation of the relationship of the
prophets to the law of Moses sheds a very interesting light on the
whole question of the origin, and early composition, of the Old
Testament canon. If the Deuteronomic movement lies at the heart
of the emergence of a canonical *torah* in Israel, as seems in every
way to have been the case,[29] then we must also consider seriously

---

[28] Cf. I. Engnell, *Critical Essays on the Old Testament*, p. 174, for this
connection between the prophets and the Deuteronomic movement.

[29] Cf. my comments in *God's Chosen People*, London, 1968, pp. 89 ff.

he implications of the Deuteronomic statements about the
prophets as witnessing to a collection of prophetic literature which
was also believed to share in this special authority. M. Noth has
contended very strongly and convincingly for the view that the
book of Deuteronomy was incorporated into the Deuteronomic
History,[30] so that the authority of the former was also carried
over, by implication, into the latter. The history of Israel's response
to the law in the age of the monarchy bore a special authoritative
witness to later generations of Israelites, which found expression
in joining the account of that history to the law itself. Furthermore,
the contention set out above that 2 Kings 17:13f. makes reference
to the work of the classical prophets suggests that these also were
regarded as possessing a special authority related to that of the
orah of Moses. Thus, in principle, both the Former Prophets
and a significant part of the Latter Prophets were considered to
share in the authority which belonged to the law of Moses. This
no doubt fell short of the very far-reaching authority which the
idea of an Old Testament canon was ultimately to imply, but it
none the less represents a very significant step towards it. What is
striking is that it witnesses to a conception of 'the Law and the
Prophets' which set them side by side as sharing together in this
special 'canonical', or 'proto-canonical', authority. Instead of
indicating a growth of the Old Testament canon which began
with the Law and added the Prophets to this as a later, secondary
stage, it suggests rather a very early joining together of 'the Law
and the Prophets', each of which subsequently underwent a good
deal of expansion and further editorial development. The question
of the priority of the Law or the Prophets, therefore, which is of
quite considerable importance for an overall theological evaluation
of the Old Testament, is set in a fresh light.

The development in Israel of this Deuteronomic conception of
the role of the prophet marks a significant aspect of the general
discussion of the relationship of the prophets to tradition. Whereas
this discussion rightly starts from a concern with the religious
traditions which underlie the prophetic preaching, it must
necessarily proceed to consider how the prophet himself became
a figure of tradition. As O. H. Steck shows, by New Testament
times the prophet had become the martyr-hero of a surprisingly
stereotyped portrait.[31] With the Old Testament the Deuteronomic

[30] M. Noth, *Überliegerungsgeschichtliche Studien I*, pp. 14ff., 94f.
[31] O. H. Steck, *Israel und das gewaltsame Geschick der Propheten*, pp. 20 ff.

picture of the prophet's role, as shown by Deuteronomy 18:15, 1
and 2 Kings 17:13–14, shows how a markedly stylized an
'traditional' picture of the prophet and his role had come to b
drawn by the sixth century B.C. This viewed him as a preacher c
torah and a spokesman of the covenant between Yahweh an
Israel. This stereotyping tendency undoubtedly also had it
connections with the redactional activity which produced collec
tions of the individual prophetic sayings into books. Thus, fo
example, we have noted earlier how a particular understanding o
the prophet's role is revealed by the terms of the propheti
commission which are woven into the call-narratives of Isaiah
Jeremiah and Ezekiel. Much more than this, however, sucl
insights as we have been able to gain into this development of
tradition concerning the prophet's role suggests some valuabl
guidelines to the ordering and redactional composition of th
prophetic books: the juxtaposition of threats of disaster witl
promises of restoration, the conception of an Israel embracin
both Northern and Southern Kingdoms, and a strong interest i
the future restoration of both under a Davidic king. All thes
point to a particular theological interpretation of the role of th
prophet. Nor should we forget the strong interest in the popula
rejection of the prophet's warnings and threats, with its connectio
with the phenomenon of 'false' prophecy, and the implications c
this for Israel's understanding of itself and of God's revelation t
it. In all of this we must certainly accept that, in spite of th
admitted silence of the eighth-century prophets about Yahweh'
covenant with Israel, it was within a framework of covenan
theology and ideas that the main lines of this traditional portrai
of the prophet came to be drawn. In spite of the many tension
and inconsistencies which this involved the circles which preserve
the traditions of the prophets and their preaching viewed then
against a background of covenant ideas which set their preachin
in a markedly new light. The immediate historical backgroun
has been supplemented with a much wider range of materi
regarding Israel's origin and vocation which had come to b
regarded as necessary and relevant. The preaching of the prophet
was given a deeper dimension, and this dimension is broadl
summed up in the main lines of Deuteronomic covenant theolog
The importance of this redactional interest makes it unsatisfactor
to attempt to understand the transmission and editing of th
prophetic sayings simply as the work of disciples, as though eacl

prophet's preaching was remembered solely within a circle which he had originated. The substantial points of similarity between the redaction of so many of the prophets, and the relationship of this to the Deuteronomic interpretation of the prophet's role in Israel show that a wider activity is evident here. This does not mean that such redaction has been a uniform process, or is the work of one single group, but only that substantial points of connection and similarity in the overall process is evident.

We may conclude by noting that the prophet himself became a figure of tradition in the Old Testament in quite a surprising way, and that the consequences of this conventionalized portrait are certainly to be seen in the way in which the sayings of the prophets have been preserved and interpreted. Not least is this fact of considerable relevance to the emergence in Judaism of a canon of prophecy which was set alongside the canon of the *torah*. Both 'the Law and the Prophets' came to acquire an authority related to the belief in the existence of a covenant between Yahweh and Israel. Certainly, also, the way in which this portrait of the prophet and his fate is applied to Jesus in the New Testament is yet a further indication of the importance of tracing and understanding its development.

5

The Prophets and the Nations

In the narrative recounting Jeremiah's call to be a prophet, Yahweh commissions him to his office by affirming that even before his birth he had been appointed 'a prophet to the nations' (Jer. 1:5). This wide international reference for the prophet's ministry is given further expression in that the book of Jeremiah contains a collection of oracles against foreign nations (Jer. 46–51). Though there are reasons for doubting that all these oracles come from Jeremiah himself, this collection of prophecies against foreign powers must be viewed in connection with similar collections in Amos (1–2), Isaiah (13–23) and Ezekiel (25–32). Furthermore, the prophecies of Nahum against Nineveh and Obadiah against Edom must also be regarded as belonging to this category of prophecies. Prophecy in Israel, therefore, contained this type of oracle concerning foreign nations and cities as a well-established category, and collections of such oracles represent a substantial and significant part of the prophetic literature. For a number of reasons the importance of these oracles has often been underestimated in studies of the message of the prophets, not least because of the complex historical questions which they pose, and because they reflect less directly on the religious life of Israel. Yet their very presence in the prophetic books is a pointer to a conception of Yahweh which saw him as more than simply the national God of Israel and to an awareness that the prophet's task was not only a ministry within Israel, but one which ranged beyond it to consider the destiny of other nations of the world.

In the correspondence referring to the activities and sayings of prophets at Mari on the Euphrates, dating from towards the end of the first half of the second millennium B.C., we find references to prophetic utterances which are to be compared to these Israelite prophecies against foreign powers. In one of the letters recounting a message that a prophet had given[1] we learn that a pronouncement had been made of the coming downfall of Hammurabi. This represented a threat against the foreign people of Babylon, the content of which was communicated to Zimri-lim the king of Mari because of its significance for his kingdom which was at war with Babylon. Thus the threat to the foreign power had a direct bearing on the life of the prophet's own people. This suggests that this kind of oracle against a foreign power was a rather round-about way of conveying a message of assurance and deliverance to the prophet's compatriots. A threat of doom against the one implied a promise for the other. In some of the Old Testament prophecies of this type a situation of this kind may be presupposed where the prophet is in effect threatening doom on peoples or cities with whom Israel or Judah is at war. It would be wrong, however, to assume that the situation was always as straightforward as this, and that the foreign power addressed in the prophecy was necessarily at war with Israel, or was in some way regarded as an immediate enemy. We shall see that a much wider range of possibilities must be considered here in connection with the way in which these prophecies were thought to function. Nevertheless, the fact that early prophecy outside the Old Testament sometimes took the form of a proclamation concerning the fate of foreign nations provides a significant indication of its character, and makes it clear that an international concern was not a late and secondary development within prophecy in general.

In the Old Testament we have a tradition about the activity of an early Moabite prophet named Balaam, who was in the service of Balak, king of Moab (Num. 22–24). When called upon to pronounce a curse against Israel we are informed that he uttered promises of Israel's greatness (Num. 23:7–10; 18–24; 24:3–9; 5–19). These promises show signs of later nationalistic aspirations of Israel, particularly relevant to David's time, so that there is doubt about how authentically they record the sayings of the Moabite Balaam. Nevertheless, the picture drawn of Balaam's activity is of a prophet who was fully trusted by the Moabite king and apparently retained by him, and whose job it was to proclaim

---

[1] Cf. F. Ellermeier, *Prophetie in Mari und Israel* (Theologische und orientalistische Arbeiten I), Herzberg, 1968, pp. 40 ff., 45 f., 137 and 142 f.; A. Malamat, 'Prophetic Revelations in New Documents from Mari and the Bible', *Geneva Congress Volume* (SVT XV), Leiden, 1966, pp. 214–19.

EP

threats against the king's enemies and to curse them. That w
also have preserved other sayings ascribed to Balaam containing
threats against Amalek (Num. 24:10), the Kenites (Num 24:21–2
and invaders from Kittim (Philistines? . . .) (Num. 24:23–4
provides further evidence of the importance of an interest in the
fate of foreign nations and peoples in early prophecy. N. K
Gottwald has claimed with justification that the form of the oracle
against a foreign nation was one of the earliest, if not the earliest
form of Hebrew prophecy.[2]

Certainly the picture that arises from this evidence of the Mar
correspondence and the Old Testament traditions about Balaam
is one in which a concern with the fate of foreign powers fell full
within the compass of a prophet's ministry. Thus there need b
no surprise that the narratives about Elijah point to his having
taken a very active interest in the political affairs of the Aramaea
kingdom of Damascus (1 Kings 19:15–18).

When we examine the various Old Testament collections o
prophecies concerning foreign nations and cities we find, no
unexpectedly, that they consist for the main part of threatening
announcements of doom, often, but not always, accompanied by
motive explaining the reason for the judgement that is to befal
the particular nation or city concerned. In some cases this motiv
appears to be the primary point of departure, so that the prophec
is in effect an affirmation that God will not leave certain specifie
offences unpunished. How this will take place is sometimes lef
rather imprecise. In other cases the motive appears to be a rathe
secondary feature and employs rather traditional and broa
assertions, most notably of *hybris* against God. Thus not only d
many of the threats have a particular interest in relation to th
complex network of international affairs and diplomacy tha
surrounded Israel, but the motive clauses also have a distinc
religious interest in connection with ideas of divine justice and o
God's government of the world.

In the earliest literary collection of such prophecies in Amo
1:3–2:6 there are strong indications that the form of such oracles
the style of their presentation, and perhaps also the type of motiv

[2] N. K. Gottwald, *All the Kingdoms of the Earth*, New York, 1964
p. 49. Cf. also H. Gunkel in *Die Schriften des Alten Testaments* II/2
2 Aufl. 1923, p. XLVI, who sees the basic prophetic speech-forms c
threat and promise most clearly expressed in the oracles against foreig
nations.

dduced for such threats, were already well-established features of
rophetic preaching. The list of the nations dealt with: Damascus,
Philistia, Tyre, Edom, Ammon, Moab, Judah, and finally Israel,[3]
oncerns peoples that were close neighbours of Israel. The fact
hat the choice of nations dealt with reflects the nations involved
n a wide treaty network which Israel headed in the time of David
as been seen[4] as indicative of a particular politico-historical basis
or the overall structure of the prophecy. In the case of the collec-
ions of such foreign oracles in Isaiah, Jeremiah, and Ezekiel the
hoice of nations dealt with does not show any such fixed pattern,
nd is more directly determined by contemporary political con-
erns. In several, though by no means all, of these prophecies the
rophet is also conscious of threats facing his own people.

The fact that some of the nations so addressed are clearly
srael's enemies, whilst in other cases this is not so obviously so,
aises the question of the function of these oracles against foreign
owers. We must ask what relation they have to the more frequently
ound oracles addressed to the prophet's own people and spoken
lirectly to them. H. Graf Reventlow[5] argues that these oracles
gainst foreign powers function in a way directly comparable to
he prophecies proclaimed to Israel. As regards their setting he
ocates these foreign prophecies in Israel's cult, in an annual
ovenant celebration. E. Würthwein[6] also looks to Israel's cult for
he setting of these prophecies in Amos. Aside from the question
f whether or not this form of prophecy belongs to a cultic setting,
vith which we shall deal later, it is hard to see that the function
f these prophecies can be the same as to those proclaimed to
srael for the simple reason that these latter were heard by
epresentatives of the people to whom they were addressed,
vhereas it is difficult to see how this could have been true of the
rophecies against foreign nations and cities. These were apparently
reached so as to be heard by Israelites, and hardly, if at all, by

[3] Cf. H. W. Wolff, *Joel und Amos*, pp. 170f. for the arguments that the
udah oracle in its present form is certainly not authentic. Wolff also
ejects as unoriginal the oracles against Tyre and Edom. That the prophet
urns finally to deal with Israel need in no way imply that the preceding
hreats were merely 'introduction' and were not intended seriously.

[4] So G. E. Wright, 'The Nations in Hebrew Prophecy', *Encounter* 26
1965), p. 236.

[5] H. Graf Reventlow, *Das Amt Des Propheten bei Amos*, p. 265.

[6] E. Würthwein, 'Der Ursprung der prophetischen Gerichtsrede',
Vort und Existenz, Göttingen, 1970, pp. 111–26.

the peoples whose downfall they proclaimed. It is certainly possibl
that at one time representatives of foreign powers at the Jerusalen
court may have participated in certain cultic celebrations in th
city, and so could have heard prophecies proclaimed there
However, there is no evidence that such occasions formed th
actual setting for prophecies of this type. In the vast majority o
cases it is either completely to be excluded, or is so improbable a
not seriously to be contemplated.

This in turn raises the question how far prophecies in Israe
may have been regarded as effective irrespective of their bein;
heard by those to whom they were addressed. Certainly, curse
may often have been uttered outside the hearing of those to whon
they were addressed, and yet have been regarded none the less a
in no way lessened in effectiveness. So also it is not only conceivable
but highly probable, that certain prophetic threats, such as fo
example Jeremiah's threats against Jehoiakim (Jer. 22:13 ff.) wer
not uttered in the hearing of the addressee, but that their effective
ness was not thought to be diminished by this. In the case of Amos
threat of the downfall of Jeroboam II (Amos 7:9, 11) the contex
makes clear that this was not spoken in the king's hearing (Amc
7:10). Even in the case of prophecies concerning people withi
Israel it was not regarded as essential that the addressee shoul
hear it. In this respect there is a certain affinity between prophec
and magic.[7] Yet we must not press this too far, and such considera
tions do not cover the broader differences of function betwee
'foreign' and 'domestic' prophecies. In the case of the foreig
nation oracles it is not simply that the addressee did not normall
hear it, but it appears to be the prophet's intention that the peopl
of Israel or Judah should hear it. In particular, the threats agains
a foreign power have an immediate relevance for the prophet'
hearers when this power constitutes a real, or potential, enemy
Thus, by a kind of reversal of function, the threats against th
enemy constitute an assurance for the prophet's hearers. Th:
seems quite clearly to be the situation in the Mari prophecie
where the threats against Hammurabi, the king of Babylor
function, and are apparently intended to function, as an assuranc

---

[7] Cf. G. Fohrer, 'Prophetie und Magie', *Studien zur alttestamentlich*
Prophetie (1949–65) (BZAW 99), Berlin, 1967, pp. 242–64, especiall
pp. 252–7 for the significance of this in regard to the prophetic word ar
its effect, and pp. 257–61 for the relationship of this to the oracles again
foreign nations.

to Zimri-lim, the king of Mari. In consequence of this S. Erlands-son[8] takes the view that the Old Testament foreign nation oracles always function in this way, and are really intended as an assurance to Israel. This certainly seems to be the case in several of the prophecies of this type. Thus, for example, the satirical lament for the death of the king of Babylon in Isaiah 14 appears to attain its significance in this way if it is to be dated to the time when Israel was suffering under Babylonian domination.[9] This also is the case with the threats of the coming downfall of Babylon (Jer. 50-1), which are probably to be placed late in the exilic age, when Judah was still under Babylonian domination. Yet not all the Old Testament oracles against foreign powers can be said to function in this way, at least not very obviously. In the case of the collection of oracles against the nations in Amos (Amos 1-2) no immediate threat to Israel's political security seems to be posed by the foreign powers addressed, and the most that can be gleaned is that they are regarded as having offended against Yahweh's 'order' for the world. Significantly too the power which many scholars have regarded as beginning to pose the main threat to Israel in Amos's time—Assyria—is not included among the threatened powers and Amos' sharp concluding threat against Israel virtually precludes a note of assurance alongside this. Similarly, and far more surprisingly, in the collection of foreign nation oracles in Ezekiel there is none foretelling the downfall of Babylon, the great enemy of Judah in Ezekiel's lifetime, in spite of the many important prophecies offering assurance and hope of restoration to Judah. In the case of the Amos oracles, as also in the case of Ezekiel's bitter oracles against Ammon, Moab, and Philistia (Ezek. 25), a strong element of moral indignation seems strongly to the fore. A deep sense of moral outrage on the part of the people of Judah cries out for vindication, and leads to threats against those who have become enemies of the prophet's people, even though no immediate prospect appears of this being trans-lated into military or political action by Judah or any other power.

Particularly interesting are the cases of the oracles against

---

[8] S. Erlandsson, *The Burden of Babylon*, pp. 65 f.

[9] N. K. Gottwald, *All the Kingdoms of the Earth*, pp. 175f., argues that the original (Isaianic) poem of Is. 14:4b–21 was composed for the death of Sargon (705 B.C.), and that the present introduction and conclusion in Is. 14:4a, 22–3, which applies it to the king of Babylon, was 'a re-appropriation of Isaiah's original poem by an exilic writer'.

Egypt, in Isaiah (Is. 19:1–15), Jeremiah (Jer. 46) and Ezekiel (Ezek. 29–32). In what are the most probable periods to which these respective oracles are to be located it is most likely that Egypt was looked upon as a potential ally of Judah, first against the Assyrians and then against the Babylonians. Thus these prophecies cannot be said to function as offering assurance of salvation to Judah by pronouncing the downfall of its enemy. Rather they would gain their political relevance by warning Judah's politicians not to rely upon Egypt for military support, since that potential ally will itself fall. This seems very clearly to underlie Ezekiel's oracles against Egypt where the progress of Nebuchadnezzar's armies against this nation is followed with careful interest. Instead of these prophecies offering any assurance to the prophet's hearers, they would rather serve to disabuse them of any premature or false, assurance. We cannot therefore force these foreign nation oracles into one mould by claiming that they consistently function as a kind of assurance for Israel. Sometimes they do, but often they do not. In other cases the degree to which the prophet's hearers would have felt any immediate and direct involvement in the fate of the nation addressed is quite obscure. It is very noteworthy that in the case of the powerful satirical oracles of Ezekiel against Tyre (Ezek. 26–28) virtually no reference at all is made to the historical relationship between Tyre and Israel. In this respect they contrast with Amos' oracle against Tyre (Amos 1:9). Instead, the city's downfall is threatened and justified as a punishment for its incalculable *hybris* against God. We cannot, it seems, assert for the foreign nation oracles any one function, either by aligning them very closely with the 'domestic' prophecies against Israel and Judah and regarding them as straightforward threats, or by seeing them as veiled pronouncements of assurance for Israel and Judah. This latter element is sometimes found, but it is also often demonstrably lacking. At best we must see these prophecies as forming a *genre* of their own.

The presence of these foreign nation oracles in each of the three large prophetic collections of Isaiah, Jeremiah, and Ezekiel indicate well enough the importance that was felt to attach to the task of the prophet as Yahweh's spokesman on international affairs. Even allowing that an extensive editorial work has been devoted to these oracles, and that material from after the prophet's own time has been added to them, they preclude our viewing the divine commission to the prophet in terms solely of a ministry within Israel

They also reveal a conception of Yahweh which was in no way content to regard him simply as the national God of Israel. That certain strata of tradition contributed to the form and content of these foreign nation oracles cannot be doubted. Certainly, a number of points have very readily attracted attention in this direction.

In the oracle against the nations in Amos 1:3–2:6 the invective by which the threatened punishment upon each of the nations addressed is justified takes the form of an accusation of having committed an atrocity against another nation, which in most cases is Israel. Some obscurity regarding the precise historical context of these crimes remains, but the indications are that they had all taken place long before the time of Amos, probably more than a century before. Thus it was certainly not Amos who first perceived them to be serious moral offences, but rather they represented traditional examples of inhuman conduct which Amos affirmed would be punished by Yahweh. The sense of moral outrage had been long felt, and what was distinctive in Amos was the use to which such grim memories were put. The rhetorical structure of this prophecy in Amos, with its distinctive stylizing as a number saying 'For three transgressions and for four . . .', whilst in fact only one example of such a transgression then follows, also reveals an element of traditional formalizing.[10]

When we look at the large collections of foreign nation oracles in Isaiah, Jeremiah and Ezekiel there are a number of striking features about the reasons given for the coming punishments that are threatened. Some features which we might have expected to be very prominent are surprisingly set in the background. Thus, for example, offences perpetrated against Israel are not as prominent as we might have expected, nor is idolatry especially singled out as an affront to Yahweh. This latter offence is treated as much more blameworthy by the prophets when it is committed by Israel. Instead, pride, especially in its distinctive religious form as *hybris*—lifting oneself up against God—is most strikingly castigated.[11] Such *hybris* is seen to manifest itself in trade, in military splendour, in the desire to rule over others, and even in the elaborate ideology of divine kingship.[12]

[10] See below, p. 77, for the claim that this particular form of the number saying represents a Wisdom motif.

[11] Is. 14:12 ff. (Babylon); 16:6 (Moab); 23:6–12 (Tyre); Jer. 48:28–33 (Moab); Ezek. 28:1 ff. (Tyre); 31:1 ff. (Egypt); 32:1 ff; 12 ff. (Egypt).

[12] Ezek. 28:2 ff., 12 ff.

There can be little doubt that these strong elements of similarity
in the invective against foreign nations and cities is the consequence
of a particular tradition about Yahweh's concern with them. Over
all, in their presence in the larger prophetic collections and in their
formal structure and content, there is ample evidence to show that
oracles against foreign nations formed a significant part of the
preaching of the Old Testament prophets. Furthermore, the form
and character of these prophecies shows that they did not first
appear with the advent of written prophecy in the eighth century
B.C., nor should we suppose that the great classical prophets were
alone in turning their attention to foreign nations. In fact, the
threats of judgement upon nations who were at times enemies of
Israel suggests that such foreign nation oracles were a conventional
part of the established scope of prophecy in Israel. They may thus
shed light on the preaching of the cultic prophets who are sometimes regarded as having consistently proclaimed salvation for
Israel, and who therefore may reasonably be supposed to have
proclaimed threats against Israel's enemies. Certainly, a number
of features relating to the prophetic concern with tradition come
to the fore in a study of these oracles against foreign powers.

The question arises whether the entire category of such foreign
nation oracles belonged to any one special sphere of Israel's life.
Two main possibilities have presented themselves: either the
setting of these oracles has been looked for in the traditions of
Israel's cult, or it has been sought in the institution of the holy
war. These possibilities are not mutually exclusive since a very
prominent cultic activity formed a part of the praxis relating to the
holy war. Thus it is possible to combine the argument for a setting
in the cultus with the view that the situation that they presuppose
is that of the holy war.

So far as Israel's cultus is concerned we may note a number of
possibilities. A. Bentzen suggested that Amos' oracle against
foreign nations represented a distinctive type of prophecy which
had its ultimate origin in execration oaths such as are found in
certain ancient Egyptian texts.[13] In these the nation's enemies were
dramatically cursed with a view to bringing about their downfall.
E. Würthwein has further developed this suggestion by arguing
that such threatening acts towards foreign powers formed a part
of the preaching of cultic prophets in Israel, and had a special

[13] A. Bentzen, 'The Ritual Background of Amos 1:2–2:16', *OTS* 8
(1950), pp. 85–99.

place in the great Israelite Autumn Festival when Israel reaffirmed Yahweh's sovereignty and the overthrow of his enemies.[14] Thus, by adopting such a form of prophecy, Amos was adopting the guise of a cultic prophet, only to relinquish it by turning his threats immediately against Israel. Other scholars also have suggested that cultic prophecy was particularly concerned with affirming the salvation of Israel so that threats against the nation's enemies may be regarded as indicating such a cultic setting.

The difficulty with all these claims is that, although we do have in the Psalms several indications that Israel's cultus concerned itself with political events, and with proclaiming threats against Israel's and Judah's enemies as a part of a general affirmation of Yahweh's rule over Israel and the nations, there is nothing to indicate that this was an exclusively cultic concern. So many areas of life were touched by political interests of this kind that prophecy inevitably reflected this, with the result that, in itself, a concern with international affairs and the fate of Israel's neighbours and enemies in prophetic sayings does not necessarily point to a cultic setting. More fruitful has been the recognition that various themes and motifs transmitted in the cultus have provided material and structural elements within the prophecies against foreign powers. Without accepting, therefore, that the cultus provided the primary and immediate context for the prophecies against foreign nations and cities it is possible to see how certain individual themes which were transmitted in the cult came to play a role in them.

Foremost among such themes we must note the portrayal of a conflict between Yahweh and certain unnamed foreign powers. This 'conflict with the nations' motif appears prominently in certain Psalms, especially the Zion psalms (Pss. 46: 8–10; 48:4–8; 76:1–6), but also in the royal psalm for a king's coronation (Ps. 2:9–11). That this motif belonged especially to the distinctive Jerusalem ideology centring on Mount Zion should not be doubted but its appearance also in a royal psalm shows its connection with the wider political order of Jerusalem and Judah. Most striking in the poetic accounts of this victory of Yahweh is the lack of any precise identification of the enemies. They are simply 'nations' or kingdoms', or even 'the kings of the earth'. In this respect the tradition is vague and obscure, and certainly its origin cannot be

[14] E. Würthwein, 'Der Ursprung der prophetischen Gerichtsrede', *Vort und Existenz*, Göttingen, 1970, pp. 111–26. Cf. also H. Graf Reventlow, *Das Amt des Propheten bei Amos*, pp. 56 ff.

traced to any known historical event. On the contrary, as many
scholars since Mowinckel[15] have noted, it is a distinctively cultic
theme. The precise nature of its origin is very much a matter of
debate. Both S. Mowinckel and A. R. Johnson[16] have put forward
the view that it represents a recasting of the mythological motif of
a divine conflict with the monster of chaos. In a distinctively
historical form the power of chaos is replaced by unnamed hostile
nations. H. M. Lutz[17] has sought to emphasize more strongly its
relationship to the tradition of the holy war in Israel and Judah,
but, along with Mowinckel, Johnson and several other scholars,
has argued that such a motif is to be traced back to the pre-Israelite
cultus of Jerusalem devoted to the deity El-Elyon.[18] There is room
for a variety of speculations here, and probably more weight than
has often been allowed should be placed on the connection of this
motif with the political structure of David's kingdom, involving
Israelite suzerainty over a number of vassal kingdoms. This was
certainly not the case in the pre-Israelite city of Jersualem, which
had previously been under vassalage to Egypt as the El-Amarna
letters make plain. This suggests that the motif may owe more to
an Israelite religious interpretation of the suzerainty structure
found in Egyptian imperialism than to the local, and politically
less influential, cult of the Jebusite El-Elyon. In any case the
unsettled debate about the origin of 'the conflict with the nations'
motif does not detract from the importance of its influence upon

[15] S. Mowinckel, *Psalmenstudien* II, rep. 1962, pp. 126ff.; cf. *The
Psalms in Israel's Worship*, I, Oxford, 1962, pp. 143ff.; J. H. Hayes
'The Tradition of Zion's Inviolability', *JBL* 82 (1963), pp. 419–26.

[16] A. R. Johnson, *Sacral Kingship in Ancient Israel*, 2nd ed. Cardiff
1967, pp. 92ff.

[17] H. M. Lutz, *Jahwe, Jerusalem und die Völker* (WMANT 27)
Neukirchen, 1968, pp. 173ff.

[18] Cf. H. M. Lutz, op. cit., pp. 174ff.; H. J. Kraus, *Psalmen* (BKA'
XV, 1), II, Neukirchen, 1960, pp. 197–205. F. Stolz, *Strukturen und
Figuren im Kult von Jerusalem* (BZAW 118), Berlin, 1970, pp. 86 f
S. Erlandsson, *The Burden of Babylon*, p. 66, suggests that it would b
more realistic to seek a connection with the coronation ritual, and point
to Ps. 2:8–11; 110:1. For this latter point we may also compare th
footnote in H. M. Lutz, op. cit., pp. 175–6, where he suggests a connec
tion between the Zion theme of Yahweh's defeat of his enemies and th
coronation ritual. Lutz, in fact, appears to regard this Zion theme o
'the conflict with the nations' as an amalgam of pre-Israelite (El-Elyon
local traditions, royal ideology and a recasting of the tradition of th
holy war (H. M. Lutz, op. cit., pp. 190ff.).

Israelite prophecy.[19] In this regard by far the most significant material is to be found in the book of Isaiah, where, as S. Erlandsson has shown,[20] the Zion ideology, and with it especially the motif of Yahweh's victory over the nations, provides a central theme which runs through all the Isaianic prophecies against foreign nations. Even allowing for a more substantial measure of later editorial redaction than Erlandsson does, the authentic ring of this Zion ideology from the lips of Isaiah forbids that we should hastily dismiss these sayings as inauthentic and only applicable to an age long after the eighth century of Isaiah. Certainly here the earlier tradition of Yahweh's conflict with nations that threatened Israel appears to have provided the prophet with a perspective from which to view the political events of his day. Similarly, the prophetic portrayal of a pilgrimage of the nations to Zion and the advent of a reign of peace among them ((Is. 2:2–4 = Mic. 4:1–4) reflects features from this older Zion motif. The content of the oracles against foreign nations, especially in Isaiah, therefore, shows a significant contact with the Zion theme which constituted an important area of tradition preserved and proclaimed in the Jerusalem cult. This falls far short, however, of demonstrating that the cultus provided the setting for all the prophetic oracles against foreign powers, or for the original type of such oracles, out of which the form and pattern of our extant prophecies may have been drawn. That the foreign nation oracles have points of contact with Israel's cultus is certain, but it is far from clear that this cultus provided their immediate setting.

The second possibility which scholars have explored as the setting of these prophecies has been the tradition of the holy war.[21] The narratives of the Israelite settlement in Palestine show a marked awareness of a conception of warfare in which Yahweh led the armies of Israel and fought on their behalf, thus making fighting itself a sacred activity surrounded by certain holy obligations and restraints. The appearance of a number of rules for the conduct of such a holy war in the book of Deuteronomy can best be taken as an indication that Josiah attempted to resurrect the national militia of Israel, with its attachment to a holy war ideology, after

[19] S. Erlandsson, op. cit., pp. 103–5.   [20] Ibid., *passim*.
[21] Cf. J. H. Hayes, 'The Usage of Oracles against Foreign Nations in Ancient Israel', *JBL* 87 (1968), pp. 81–92; G. H. Jones, *An Examination of Some Leading Motifs in the Prophetic Oracles against Foreign Nations*, unpublished doctoral dissertation, Bangor, 1970.

the exhaustion of state funds precluded the maintenance of a large professional standing army. Altogether there is ample evidence that the ideology of the holy war was an important feature of early Israelite life, and that even in the seventh century B.C. it remained an influential aspect of Israelite thought and life.

Since the prophecies against foreign nations refer, in a number of instances, to nations which were, or had been, Israel's enemies it is attractive to look for connections between those oracles which declare Yahweh's judgement on such nations and the institutions and ideas concerned with the holy war in which Israel saw Yahweh as its leader in battle. Thus it is tempting to see in the holy war ideology an essential part of the background of these prophecies. The influence of such holy war traditions on prophecy could then be examined in several directions. G. von Rad[22] has argued for its importance as the background to Isaiah's conception of faith, and his pupil R. Bach[23] has sought to trace its impact on the form of certain prophetic speeches summoning Israel into battle, or to flee from the field of battle. That a considerable priestly activity related to Israel's conduct in the holy war is shown by references in Deuteronomy regulating Israel's actions (Deut. 20:1 ff.), and it is in every way likely that prophets also were concerned in such situations. The oracular type utterances in certain psalms which point to the king's leadership of the army into battle (Ps. 20:6–8; 21:8–13; 91) also suggest that the holy war ideology, with its heavy implication that Israel's enemies are Yahweh's enemies and that victory comes from Yahweh, was important to the preaching of some prophets. Here again it is particularly attractive to think of the activity of cultic prophets, and it may well be that their work is reflected in Psalm 91. That certain cultic prophets should have been employed, like Balaam of Moab, to threaten the nation's enemies is quite plausible. Yet the holy war can hardly have provided the setting for all our preserved foreign nation oracles since, as we have already noted, they cannot be consistently regarded as directed at Israel's enemies with a view to providing assurance for Israel. In some cases the foreign nations are undoubtedly Israel's enemies, but in other cases they are not. It is a reasonable conjecture that the category of an oracle against a foreign nation owes something to the ideology of the holy war, and

---

[22] G. von Rad, *Old Testament Theology*, II, pp. 159 ff.

[23] R. Bach, *Die Aufforderungen zur Flucht und zum Kampf im alttestamentlichen Prophetenspruch* (WMANT 9), Neukirchen, 1962.

perhaps the type in general arose in a situation of military action when national, political and religious aspirations were very keenly felt. The evidence from the Mari correspondence and the picture given by the Old Testament of Balaam's role would not be out of line with this. Yet by the time of the emergence of written prophecy in the eighth century B.C. the type of the foreign nation oracle would no longer appear to be directly linked with such a setting. Amos did not begin by preaching against Israel's contemporary enemies, and the impression is given that oracles against foreign powers were neither restricted to the military camp nor to a time of actual warfare. Whatever the category of such prophecy may once have owed to the ideas and practices of the holy war, therefore, must have already receded into the background. In any case the holy war was not a fixed institution, but must have provided a variety of impulses and activities which were married to the developing life of Israel's cult and society. Thus it is possible that the holy war ideology has influenced the content, and perhaps even the form, of some oracles against foreign nations and cities, although we cannot confidently claim that it provides the setting of all the foreign nation oracles. That military situations should have provided an evocative setting for certain phrases and speech-forms such as calls to attack, or to flee, which have then been utilized by some prophets should not surprise us. This does not mean, however, that the holy war provided a sufficiently self-contained context for it to be regarded as the setting of all such prophecies. It was in any case inevitable that, since the prophets were presenting threats of impending military conflict and defeat, they should have drawn upon verbal images and conventions of war which give life and vigour to their prophecies. All in all, therefore, there is no very substantial ground for accepting that the holy war provided the essential setting for prophecies against foreign nations. Many prophecies of this type do not presuppose that Israel is either actually, or potentially, at war with the nation concerned, and other factors weigh against associating the prophecies too closely with the holy war. We have already seen that a number of connections link some elements of the foreign nation oracles with Israel's cult, and this must have been a continuing cultic activity, and not one that was only called upon in time of war. The likelihood is therefore that oracles against foreign powers were also a continuing aspect of Israel's religious life, and were not a phenomenon found only in time of war. If such oracles first appeared in time of

war they must soon have developed quite outside their original
setting. Further, the content of the invective which is frequently
used in these oracles to explain and justify the coming judgement
shows little obvious or direct contact with ideas of the holy war.
Instead, there is clear evidence that such invective has been the
subject of a developing tradition of its own which relates very
broadly to religious, cultural, and political aspects concerning the
nations addressed.

That any one sphere of Israel's life, the royal court, the cultus or
the military organization of the state with its inheritance of holy
war ideology, formed the exclusive setting of the category of the
oracles against foreign powers cannot be regarded as established.
Rather we must regard these prophecies as a distinctive genre of
their own which drew from many aspects of Israel's life. If, in its
origin, the genre owed a particular debt to the ideology of the holy
war, so that it had its earliest setting on the field of battle, it must
quickly have lost this original restricted context. Such a category
of prophecy reveals a broad development with connections with
several areas of Israel's life, and the category in general displays
clear signs of having been subjected to an interesting and quite
distinctive tradition of development.

6

Wisdom, Prophecy, and Apocalyptic

One particular facet of Israel's intellectual heritage has come to acquire a special prominence in recent study. This is the pursuit of wisdom, which Israel shared with her near-eastern neighbours, even though the actual concept of wisdom itself appears to have no exactly comparable counterpart either in Egypt or Mesopotamia. Wisdom found an early home in Israel, and its intellectual vitality and moral persuasiveness made it an important aspect of Israelite culture. Because of its relationship to the activities of scribes and to the influential sphere of the royal court it appears to have given rise at a fairly early stage to literary collections, and to have represented a very distinctive movement with a number of characteristic themes and ideas. Before it is possible to look at the influence which such wisdom traditions may have had upon prophecy it is necessary to note the very different views regarding the character and setting of wisdom which constitute a considerable debate in modern Old Testament scholarship.[1] Most prominent here is the divergence between those scholars who see wisdom as primarily a court activity, designed to promote the interests of statecraft, and those who regard it as a more domestic pursuit, the roots of which lie in the tribal and clan structure of society such as pertained in early Israel. Certainly, differing features of wisdom show particular relevance to one or other such spheres. The practical moral advice, the characteristic form of address 'my son', and the broad concern with behaviour in the home and in society in general show the popular, and often rural, background of much proverbial wisdom. On the other hand the sophisticated outlook of many proverbs, the favourable attitude towards the monarchy,

[1] Cf. R. E. Murphy, 'Form Criticism and Wisdom Literature', *CBQ*, 31 (1969), pp. 475–83.

the concern to 'get on' in the world and to seek social advancement, together with the ascription of some collections of proverbs to royal figures, all show an association with the royal court. In particular the traditional ascription of much of the Old Testament wisdom literature to Solomon suggests that this king, as a part of the administrative organization of his empire, established a court 'Wisdom School' in Jerusalem where young members of the court circle could receive training before taking office in the state administration. Such a school would certainly have reflected a degree of Egyptian influence in Solomon's time, and such influence appears to be evident in a number of features of Israelite wisdom. Even so, it is too narrow a view to limit all wisdom to a setting in the court, and to relate its interest too narrowly to the sphere of statecraft. Much that was domestic and concerned with everyday occasions of moral decision was basic to wisdom.

If this is the case, then we cannot suppose that wisdom was the perquisite of any one class of people in ancient Israel, who constituted the circle of the wise, or that it belonged pre-eminently to any one particular professional group. Although, no doubt, the administrative officers of the state were drawn from the wealthier families who considered that they were especially endowed with wisdom, and were therefore especially concerned to cultivate it, there is no reason to believe that they either possessed a monopoly of wisdom, or that less privileged members of the population did not also see in the acquisition of wisdom a useful and desirable goal. Perhaps it is most of all in the activities of professional scribes, of which a considerable number would have found employment in the court and the royal administration, that wisdom came closest to being associated with one particular professional class in Israel. Thus the court scribes would have provided a significant agency for the collection and literary recording of proverbial wisdom both from within Israel and abroad.

This openness in the debate about the central characteristics of early wisdom has made for a considerable variety of interpretations regarding the influence which such wisdom traditions may have had upon the great prophets of the Old Testament. J. Fichtner noted a number of words and themes in the prophet Isaiah which he believed showed the influence of wisdom thinking upon the

---

[2] J. Fichtner, 'Jesaja unter den Weisen', *Gottes Weisheit. Gesammelt Studien zum A.T.*, ed. K. D. Fricke, Stuttgart, 1965, pp. 18–26 and 'Jahwes Plan in der Botschaft des Jesaja', ibid., pp. 27–43.

the prophet. He suggested as an explanation of this that Isaiah had been brought up as a young man in the court circle of Jerusalem, with its emphasis upon wisdom, and that, after receiving his call to be a prophet he had turned against such wisdom ideas. Thus the use of these wisdom ideas in Isaiah is taken to indicate certain features about Isaiah's personal background, on the understanding that the pursuit of wisdom was a special concern of the court circle and its involvement in politics. However, since a similar sharp antipathy to wisdom is also evident in Jeremiah, the same explanation ought to apply here also, although in fact it is virtually impossible to uphold this in the face of Jeremiah's undoubted priestly background (Jer. 1:1). In fact, both in Isaiah and Jeremiah the sharp collision between the word of God preached by the prophet and the 'plan' or 'counsel' pursued by their opponents and ascribed to wisdom has been used by W. McKane to indicate a much wider confrontation between the prophetic word and the pursuit of wisdom, which McKane sees primarily as a means of statecraft.[3] Thus McKane sees a fundamental disagreement between the prophetic knowledge of God's will derived from the divine disclosure of it to prophets, and the more secular and anthropocentric reliance on the insights and precedents of wisdom which formed the natural thought world of Israel's and Judah's politicians. On such an understanding there is no room at all for any kind of positive influence from the sphere of wisdom upon the prophet. On the contrary, the use made by the prophet of the vocabulary and ideas relating to wisdom is seen as an inevitable consequence of the contrasting ideas of revelation and man's knowledge of the divine will appropriate to prophecy and wisdom respectively. Thus the prophet's challenge to Israel's reliance on wisdom is not derived from any special personal background in the study of wisdom which the prophet himself had experienced, but is a part of the unique and distinctive nature of the phenomenon of prophecy and its consciousness of a special revelation of the divine will. Viewed in these terms the collision between prophecy and wisdom must be regarded as an inevitable consequence of the quite different starting points from which each has begun. In a large measure there is presented here a deep-rooted confrontation between the secular and worldly interests of the court and the religious, and more cultically oriented interests of the prophets. Yet this is certainly to go too far. Whilst McKane's interpretations

[3] W. McKane, *Prophets and Wise Men* (SBT 44), London, 1965.

FP

of the passages in Isaiah and Jeremiah are very convincing, th
wider conclusions drawn from them are less so. That the politician
of ancient Israel claimed to base their policies on wisdom is clea
enough, but this falls far short of showing further that the earlies
Israelite wisdom was entirely secular and indifferent to the religiou
sphere. Not all wisdom was concerned with politics, nor was i
exclusively a pursuit of the court circle. Recent attention to th
sphere of popular folk wisdom offers a much wider canvas on whicl
to paint a picture of early Israelite wisdom and its characteristics
Thus, although McKane rightly opposes any over-simplifie(
conclusions about the personal background of the prophets on th
basis of their use of what is regarded as wisdom terminology an(
ideas, we cannot counter this by presenting wisdom and prophec
as two opposed spheres of understanding. There was a religiou
element in early wisdom and there was a degree of commo
interest between the two in their concern with morality and th
general order and harmony of society. Even though a measure o
tension between the two may be seen to be readily intelligible, i
was not institutionally inevitable.

This leads us on to consider the rather different approach whicl
has been made in tracing the impact of wisdom traditions upon th
prophets on the understanding that the roots of Israelite wisdon
lie in the folk ethos of its clan and tribe oriented society. Acceptin
that the origins of wisdom and its nurture in Israel go back to th
period before the introduction of a royal court and the organizatio
of the state, H. W. Wolff has sought to show that such wisdon
traditions form the spiritual background of the preaching of Amos.
Wolff sees the fundamental milieu of wisdom in the family life an(
ethos of the tribal society of early Israel, which was graduall
modified and superseded by the urban ethos of the city-stat(
society inherited from Canaan. Thus, not only is the wisdon
influence which Wolff sees in Amos a predominantly ethica
concern, but it was also representative of the old order which wa
threatened with disintegration under the impact of the transitio
to urbanized society and monarchic government. Thus, in marke(
contrast to McKane, Wolff sees this folk wisdom as built upo
presuppositions sharply differing from these of the sophisticate(

---

[4] First of all Wolff sets out his thesis in his monograph *Amos' geistig
Heimat* (WMANT 18), Neukirchen, 1964, and the consequences of hi
conclusions are applied in detail in his commentary on Amos, *Joel un(
Amos* (BKAT XIV, 2), Neukirchen, 1967.

circle of the court. Such a view of wisdom advocated by Wolff finds support in the arguments presented by E. Gerstenberger that the basic ethical demands of the decalogue and their apodictic form also originated in the sphere of such folk wisdom.[5] So, incidentally, Wolff takes up Gerstenberger's claim that the form of the woe-oracle, which is found prominently in Amos and Isaiah, was derived originally from a didactic form current in wisdom teaching.[6] It would, however, carry us too far from our immediate concern to consider the whole range of arguments and conclusions presented by Gerstenberger.

Wolff's arguments regarding the influence of folk wisdom on Amos concern the particular form of some of the prophetic sayings, certain features of vocabulary and the style of argument, and some incidental factors of which the most notable is Amos' family origin from Tekoa, where Wolff believes a distinctive tradition of skill in wisdom was kept alive.[7] Support for this he finds in 2 Sam. 14:1 ff., where Joab fetched a wise woman from Tekoa to use her verbal skill in persuading David to allow Absalom back at court. This is further connected by Wolff with the view that a special pride in the nurture of wisdom was current among the Edomites, which may also have been shared by neighbouring parts of southern Judah. We may summarize briefly Wolff's main points:

1. The use of number sayings in the oracle against the nations (Amos 1:3–2:6), which is a distinctive wisdom form of instruction. Cf. Prov. 30:15–31.
2. The use of a distinctive type of logical reasoning from effect to a prior cause in Amos 3:2–9.
3. The use of sayings cast in the woe-form, which Wolff regards as a distinctively wisdom speech-form in its origin.
4. The strong ethical concern, with a fundamental appeal to apodictic commands.

Accepting this folk wisdom as the spiritual background of Amos, Wolff sees a marked difference in character in this from the background of Hosea, which Wolff regards as more directly cultic and

---

[5] E. Gerstenberger, *Wesen und Herkunft des 'apodiktischen Rechts'* (WMANT 20), Neukirchen, 1965. Cf. also his essay, 'Covenant and Commandment', *JBL* 84 (1965), pp. 38–51.

[6] E. Gerstenberger, 'The Woe-Oracles of the Prophets', *JBL* 81 (1962), pp. 249–63; H. W. Wolff, pp. 12 ff.

[7] H. W. Wolff, pp. 53 f.

related to the traditions of certain circles of Levites. These
conclusions about the influence of folk wisdom on Amos have been
challenged by J. L. Crenshaw,[8] who argues that the particular
features in Amos which Wolff regards as indicative of folk wisdom
do not necessarily, or exclusively, originate from this sphere
Nevertheless, Crenshaw claims that the use of the theophany motif
in the 'doxologies' of the book of Amos point to the tradition of
wisdom, so that there is none the less an element of wisdom influence upon the prophet. In this, however, it is hard to see that the
argument for a special wisdom tradition lying behind Amos has
been much strengthened. Not only is there a good deal of un
certainty on the question whether the 'doxologies' were an authentic
part of the original preaching of Amos, but it is very difficult to
see why the theophany theme should have belonged primarily to
the teaching of wisdom. On the contrary, it appears very frequently
and prominently in cultic contexts. Thus the fact that the theophany
motif appears in Job, which Crenshaw takes to indicate that it had
a wisdom setting, is quite inadequate to support the claim that it
was a distinctive wisdom motif. Thus, although there is much of
value in Crenshaw's criticisms of the arguments of Wolff about the
influence of wisdom upon Amos, his own attempt to replace these
arguments by another one, based upon the connection of the
theophany theme with wisdom, and thereby to arrive at a similar
destination by a different route, is far from convincing.

In fact we may feel a considerable doubt and air of inconclusive
ness about the whole claim for a strong and influential element of
wisdom thinking underlying the book of Amos, to which various
factors contribute. From the outset we are compelled to raise the
question how we can in any case identify 'wisdom influence' in
any very precise way. Undoubtedly certain themes, and conse
quently certain units of vocabulary and idiom, tend to reappear very
frequently in the book of Proverbs and other wisdom writings. Yet
it is far from clearly being substantiated that there was a dis
tinctive technical vocabulary of wisdom which can be readily
identified.[9] In the case of the vocabulary of moral behaviour and

[8] J. L. Crenshaw, 'The Influence of the Wise upon Amos. The "Doxo
logies of Amos" and Job 5:9–16; 9:5–10', *ZAW* 79 (1967), pp. 42–5²
See also the criticisms of H. H. Schmid, 'Amos. Zur Frage nach der
"geistige Heimat" des Propheten', *Wort und Dienst*, N.F. 10 (1969)
pp. 85–103.

[9] The attempt of R. B. Y. Scott, *The Way of Wisdom*, New York
1971, pp. 121 f. to formulate a list of distinctive wisdom vocabulary

he processes of decision-making, both in politics and everyday commercial life, the situations themselves determine the words employed so that they cannot legitimately be ascribed to a particular circle, or tradition, of wisdom. Thus descriptions of moral behaviour and ethical offences are primarily dictated by the social and cultural structure of life in society, rather than by the educational endeavours of any one particular group. The identification of certain wisdom forms of speech, the proverb, the riddle, the admonition and the skilful saying, are all sufficiently broadly based and widely identifiable to mark them as part of the common oral and literary heritage belonging to a nation's whole culture. They cannot therefore be said to represent the prerogative of a special class of people, identifiable from within the nation as a whole. This particularly applies to such a rhetorical device as the number saying, which owes its use to its artistic and rhetorical effectiveness, rather than to its origin in, or usefulness to, any one particular setting in life. Thus, although we cannot altogether dismiss the affinity of certain themes, stylistic devices and vocabulary, which are found in Amos and some other prophets, to wisdom teaching, this in itself falls far short of establishing a conclusive case that they have been drawn from a specific milieu of wisdom traditions. At most they show what has long been recognized that Amos shows a variety of contacts with a religious and ethical tradition which was at home in the older, rural, and clan oriented pattern of Israelite society. To label this influence as 'wisdom' has only a partial justification, since we must allow more room than Wolff does for the orientation of some proverbial and wisdom teaching to the court. The favourable interest in the kingship of some wisdom teaching points us to a significant scribal activity in court circles, at least for the collection, if not for the origination, of such instruction, and this contrasts with the emphasis upon a setting in rural life and a clan society, which Wolff regards as implied by the presence of wisdom elements in Amos.

Arguments not altogether dissimilar from those employed by Wolff in regard to Amos are used in a study of Isaiah and wisdom by J. W. Whedbee, in which he argues for a strong influence of

quite unconvincing, because it makes no attempt to distinguish words that simply occur in wisdom contexts, from those which can be said to belong distinctively, if not exclusively, to the pursuit and teaching of wisdom. It is far from certain that such a list could be compiled even if we possessed a far greater literature from which to draw it.

wisdom traditions upon this prophet.[10] Thus, developing a line of investigation suggested by R. Fey's claim that the prophet Isaiah shows a strong familiarity with the preaching of Amos.[11] Whedbee goes on to suggest that this may be attributable to their use of common traditions of wisdom. Whedbee bases his main case for the influence of wisdom teaching upon Isaiah on the use of certain forms of speech, which he claims are proverbial in character, and the frequent appearance of what he regards as 'technical wisdom vocabulary'. He also sees in Isaiah more generally a wisdom style of speech and argumentation. To this he adds a further examination of Gerstenberger's thesis regarding the origin of the form of the woe-oracle in wisdom instruction, and suggests that, although the claim cannot be regarded as proven, it can enjoy a reasonable probability. In all this Whedbee presupposes a setting of wisdom in the wide circle of clan society and its ethos, as does Wolff, and affirms that there is no clear evidence of the existence of a wisdom school in Jerusalem.

The claims and counter-claims in regard to the influence of wisdom upon literature outside the commonly accepted wisdom books of the Old Testament can thus be seen to have developed into a substantial area of research of its own. Yet a number of particular points are especially relevant to the discussion of the influence of wisdom traditions upon the prophets, and may be noted, even though a detailed study of all the relevant passages cannot be pursued.

First of all, once we move away from accepting any especially direct connection of wisdom with any one professional class of politicians, scribes, educators or with an élite court circle, the whole setting of wisdom becomes much looser and ill-defined. Who were the wise? Did they at all constitute an identifiable group or class within society, or was not wisdom an attainment to which all might aspire?[12] The claim that the origins of wisdom are to be sought in the ethos and home life of the older tribally structured society suggests a very wide nurturing of wisdom, which could

[10] J. W. Whedbee, *Isaiah and Wisdom*, New York–Nashville, 1971.

[11] R. Fey, *Amos und Jesaja* (WMANT 12), Neukirchen, 1963, *passim*. cf. Whedbee, op. cit., pp. 20f.

[12] This is well pointed out in the valuable review of Whedbee's book by J. L. Crenshaw in *Interpretation* 26 (1972), pp. 74–7. Crenshaw comments, 'The assumption of specific wisdom influence upon a prophet rests on the premise that we know precisely what makes up both wisdom and prophecy and that each existed in isolation' (p. 75).

well have influenced very large sections of Israel and Judah. No
single identifiable circle, or class, of the wise can then readily be
posited or identified. Alongside of this, however, we must certainly
note that there is a court orientation and atmosphere in some parts
of our collections of proverbs which precludes our dismissing
altogether the role of a court scribal circle in the collecting and
disseminating of forms of wisdom instruction. Whilst the court
held no monopoly on wisdom there was undoubtedly a strong
court interest in sponsoring its pursuit, and the literary forms of
wisdom which have come down to us may owe not a little to the
editorial labours of court scribes. Nevertheless, we cannot assume
that 'the wise' formed a separate and identifiable class of people
from whom wisdom traditions might especially be derived. Thus
the claim to have found evidence of wisdom influence upon a particular prophet is only of very limited help in gaining an understanding of his particular background, since we should hardly
expect a prophet to be altogether without such influence. The
broader the picture of the setting of wisdom is shown to be, so
much the vaguer and less meaningful do the traces of wisdom in
prophecy become. There was no separate 'circle of the wise' who
might be regarded as the jealous guardians of particular wisdom-
oriented standards and instructional techniques. Thus, for
example, Whedbee's claim[13] that the connection of drunkenness
with social injustice is especially characteristic of wisdom can
hardly be upheld, and to do so is to reduce wisdom simply to the
level of commonplace moral insight. Unless we can clearly mark
off the separate boundaries of wisdom and prophecy with some
degree of confidence we can hardly expect to trace the influence
of one upon the other.

A second point should also be raised here. Some of the features
adduced by Wolff and Whedbee as specifically wisdom forms or
methods of argumentation, are in reality more in the nature of
stylistic devices than fixed oral forms. Thus we may include here
the true proverb itself (Hebrew *māshāl*), with its use of simile and
analogy, the number saying, as well as types of ironical speech and
forms of deductive reasoning which belong broadly to the realm
of rhetorical artistry, and are used more for their effect upon the
hearers, than because they are specifically appropriate to any one
setting in life. Thus most of them can be seen generally to be
didactic devices and types of artistic speech such as any public

[13] J. W. Whedbee, op. cit., p. 103.

speaker might use, and are not restricted to any one teaching situation, whether of home, court, or classroom. It would be wrong, therefore, to treat such stylistic forms as indications of direct dependence or imitation such as apply to the more rigidly kept forms of juridical speech, prophetic utterance and cultic hymns and laments where a particular life setting is presupposed. It is not surprising, therefore, that many of the features adduced by Whedbee, such as the use of proverbial sayings and types of argumentation, can be found also in other prophets, notably Hosea and Jeremiah, in such a way as to undermine altogether the argument for a special dependence of Isaiah upon wisdom. The whole thesis becomes so broad as to be of no real assistence in understanding what is distinctive of a particular prophet.

A similar unsatisfactoriness is found in the attempt to identify a technical wisdom vocabulary. Here it is very difficult to establish adequate criteria upon which useful working hypotheses can be built. Whilst there are particular themes which frequently occur in proverbial sayings and certain types of moral and immoral behaviour repeatedly draw forth the comments and criticisms of the authors of proverbs, the vocabulary itself is largely determined by the specific situation dealt with, and belongs broadly to the context of that situation. It is not, therefore, the invention of the wisdom authors, and cannot be regarded as exclusive to a small circle of people. The problem of distinguishing characteristic preferences in vocabulary usage is made all the more acute by the very limited range of literature available in the Old Testament, especially specifically wisdom literature.

Unquestionably, the most decisive material for studying the part played by wisdom traditions in the preaching of the prophets remains those passages where explicit reference is made to those who are wise, or who claim to be so, and who make use of a special wisdom. Here, the most striking passages are those to be found in the prophets Isaiah and Jeremiah to which McKane draws special attention. In these the note is consistently one of conflict, and indicates a sharp collision between the policies pursued by the ruling classes—who constituted the actual government—and those urged upon the people by the prophets in the name of Yahweh. Yet even here we have already pointed out that this collision cannot be taken to have arisen from an inherent and inevitable conflict between the secular empiricism of the politicians and the the divine word revealed to the prophets, but rather relates to the more immediate situation of the actual policies being pursued and the special warnings and threats delivered by the prophets. In principle, it is little different from the conflict between one prophet and another, which is apparent in Micah and Jeremiah, and which leads to the identification of 'false' prophets. It is the immediate situation which most clearly explains the conflict, rather than a fixed dependence on traditions which brought certain prophets face to face with men who backed up their policies with an appeal to their own wisdom and insight.

In a further direction the study of the traditions underlying prophecy and wisdom has led to a significant discussion in another, and more limited, area of Old Testament literature. This is the field of apocalyptic, which is represented in the Old Testament by the book of Daniel, and by a much wider literature in the Pseudepigrapha.

G. von Rad has set forth the claim that to view apocalyptic as a child of prophecy is completely out of the question. This represents a very marked divergence from the view of earlier scholars that apocalyptic is to be regarded as the breaking out in a new form of the eschatological hope which had earlier been proclaimed by the prophets. Apocalyptic seemed clearly to be the natural and legitimate heir of the prophets, whereas von Rad has now sought to replace this by arguing that the true seed-bed from which it has grown is that of wisdom. The arguments for this new understanding of the origin of apocalyptic are set out by von Rad briefly in the first English edition of Volume II of his *Old Testament Theology*,[14] and these arguments are further developed with greater elaboration in the fourth and subsequent German editions of this work.[15]

The main points put forward relate to the consideration that there is a marked incompatibility between the prophetic view of history and that presented by the apocalyptists. Whereas the former is distinctly confessional in character and regards the events of history as a drama revealing the acts of God, that of apocalyptic is much flatter and more mechanistic, in which the divine action manifests itself only to the last generation of Israel. The standpoint of the apocalyptists is no longer overtly the contemporary situation, as with the prophets, but an era long since past, to which the

[14] First German edition 1962, English translation by D. M. G. Stalker 1965, pp. 301–8.
[15] Munich, 1965, pp. 315 ff.

revelations of the end time are projected back as ancient pre-
dictions. Furthermore, the recognition of the advent of this end
time and its significance is not clear and open, but is hidden
beneath complex figurative addresses, elaborate code signs and
obscure dreams which need expert interpretation. The changed
attitude to history, argues von Rad, stems not from prophecy but
from wisdom. Thus we see the teaching of the wise that 'everything has its time' (Eccles. 3:1 ff.) has been developed into a great
scheme of sequential cosmic aeons, appropriate to a divinely
ordained programme of salvation. The pursuit of knowledge has
been elaborated into 'a great cosmological gnosis' in which the
agents of its apprehension and interpretation are presented, like
Daniel, as 'wise men', skilled in knowledge and the interpretation
of dreams. Nor is the earlier ethical note of wisdom dropped from
this new literary form, which has its own hortatory function. Thus
von Rad concludes that 'a great gulf' separates prophecy from
apocalyptic and that we must look to the tradition of wisdom in
order to explain the origin of the latter.

Not surprisingly a measure of protest has been raised against
this attempt to find a fresh explanation for the origins of apocalyptic, and we must note here particularly the very perceptive,
though brief, essay by P. von der Osten-Sacken.[16] He argues that,
although there are clearly markedly new features in apocalyptic
which make it a distinctive form, there are also elements which are
derived from prophecy. Thus features of Daniel 2 show a marked
dependence on Deutero-Isaiah,[17] and the material used in the
composition of Daniel 8–12 shows a dependence on prophetic
traditions, especially those concerning the Day of the Lord.[18]
Furthermore, von der Osten-Sacken argues in relation to apocalyptic itself that the horizon to which it looks is not the cosmos
and its dissolution, but history and the events which take place
within it. The presence of deterministic statements in apocalyptic
with their affinity to similar ideas expressed in wisdom literature
especially Ecclesiastes, can be understood, not from a direct
dependence of the former on the latter, but from a common
concern with God as Creator. Yet even so, we cannot altogether
discount a degree of attachment to wisdom categories in apoca

[16] P. von der Osten-Sacken, *Die Apokalyptik in ihrem Verhältnis z*
Prophetie und Weisheit (Theologische Existenz heute 157), Munich, 1969
[17] P. von der Osten-Sacken, op. cit., pp. 23 ff.
[18] P. von der Osten-Sacken, op. cit., pp. 39 ff.

lyptic, but these are not so much fundamental as supplementary. Only in the course of its development did apocalyptic adopt more and more features from wisdom. In essence apocalyptic is a late and distinctive, but none the less legitimate, form of prophecy.

Certainly the debate on this issue is far from concluded, and it may well represent a significant growing point for further research. That the attitude to wisdom and the conception of the wise man in apocalyptic is very different from that which we found earlier in the pre-exilic prophets, especially Isaiah and Jeremiah, is markedly evident. Yet there are also many features of apocalyptic which stand very close to the preaching of the earlier prophets, and which appear to derive from them. Recognizing that apocalyptic is a new and very distinctive form of literature, we must also note that it undoubtedly presupposes a passionate concern with contemporary historical events, which is very similar to that of the prophets. Furthermore it calls for a response to its message in terms of repentance and a new obedience to God which is genuinely prophetic in its tone and intensity. Thus, whatever allowance we may make for the changes that had befallen the teaching and understanding of wisdom in Judaism and the influence which it may have had upon the literature of apocalyptic, it appears neither necessary nor judicious to assert too sharp a division between prophecy and apocalyptic, and to deny the influence of the former upon the latter.

In this regard another factor must also be borne in mind. As we noted in our study of the emergence in Judaism of a stereotyped conception of the role of the prophet, there was a tendency to present the prophet as a preacher of *torah*-law, as it came increasingly to be regarded. Thus the portrayal of the prophet as a preacher of repentance, calling the people back to the Mosaic *torah* which he reaffirmed, sharply reduced the concern with the predictive elements of his prophecies. The more firmly prophecy came to subsumed under this category, so much less room was there within it for a truly flexible approach to its understanding of the future. Apocalyptic sought to recover something truly prophetic in its marked re-emphasis on prediction of the future and a fresh interest in God's ultimate concern with Israel in history. Alongside this we must set the strange caricaturing of the prophet in the book of Jonah, where again the prophet is primarily viewed as a preacher of repentance, and the sharp antipathy to prophets expressed in Zech. 13:2-6. Before we accept too readily the claim for a complete separation between the differing views of history of the prophets and apocalyptists, we must ask what had become of prophecy by the second century B.C. The unexpectedly hostile note regarding prophets which suddenly appears by this time may itself be a key towards understanding why the new form of apocalyptic literature became a spiritual necessity.

7

Conclusion

In the foregoing survey a number of aspects of the prophetic concern with, and use of, religious traditions in ancient Israel has been considered, and the attempt can now be made to formulate some conclusions. Perhaps at the outset it is useful to deal with certain broad features which will enable us to set the more detailed problems in perspective. Of such basic factors probably the most far-reaching is that 'tradition' itself in ancient Israel cannot be regarded as in any sense a uniform entity, nor as imposing a unifying pattern upon Israelite religion generally or the Old Testament prophets in particular. In this respect my earlier study, *Prophecy and Convenant*, did not allow sufficiently for the diversity of the various cultic and covenantal traditions in ancient Israel. It follows from this lack of uniformity in the religious traditions represented in the Old Testament that the prophetic encounter with them does not provide any necessary point of unity or co-ordination in the prophets' preaching. We cannot therefore use the prophetic concern with tradition as a co-ordinating factor in assembling together a theology of ancient Israel, or of the Old Testament, even though the general questions of revelation raised by this concern have a direct and important theological relevance. This undoubtedly means that we cannot treat each identifiable religious tradition in Israel, whether it was mediated through a particular cultic centre or circle of people, as itself representing a particular stratum of theology. This would be to treat each tradition as though it were a theological doctrine, which is not historically acceptable, even though distinctive traditions were evidently characterized by particular theological emphases. Thus we cannot speak of a 'Zion theology' or a 'wisdom theology', even though very distinctive theological features belong to the Zion cultus and to the pursuit of wisdom in Israel. The theological emphasis was not abstracted from the tradition, nor was it consistently appealed to in order to justify and maintain it. We cannot always assume therefore that it was the theological emphasis of the tradition which provided the prophets with their point of contact with it. In some cases, as for example with rites of sacrifice, the considerable variety of interpretations which are reflected in the Old Testament show that there was no uniform 'theology of sacrifice' current in Israel which the prophets could call upon, either positively or negatively, in their invective against those who offered sacrifices to God.

This lack of uniformity in Israel's religious traditions affects our study most directly in connection with traditions of covenant where some attempts have been made to find certain very broad patterns into which the prophetic preaching can be fitted. The most persuasive of these has been to trace an office of covenant mediator, or law speaker, with certain institutional obligations and formal characteristics of speech which are then also thought to be traceable in the prophets. In this way the most essential features of prophecy are claimed to be related to a framework of covenant ideology, with distinctive theological presuppositions. Yet great doubt attaches to the question whether such an office of covenant mediator ever existed, and, more importantly, none of the features which are adduced in support of the attempt to relate the prophets to such an office can convincingly be said to do so. They are all equally, or better, explained in other ways. The similar attempt to connect the prophets with traditions of covenant by way of reference to a covenant form based upon analogies with Near Eastern suzerainty treaties must be regarded as a failure because of the serious doubts about the validity of such analogies, and the various attempts that have been made to explain them historically as a consequence of Israelite borrowing and adaptation of the form. The case for an early adoption of this covenant form in Israel would have to be much stronger than it is for it to appear plausible that the prophets made conscious reference to it and moulded some of their prophecies upon its ideas and forms. Even if it were granted that certain circles formulated their understanding of Israel's relationship to God in this way it would not necessarily imply that the prophets followed this in their own understanding of such a relationship. In this, as in various other attempts to draw far-reaching deductions about the content of the prophetic preaching from more superficial similarities of form and vocabulary with other literature, no strong case can be made to show an underlying and uniform covenant ideology as a basis for the prophetic message or the prophet's function. Certainly in general we are not likely to arrive at a very convincing assessment of the prophetic preaching if more weight is given to uncertain evaluations of its form than to the much clearer and less equivocal statements of its content. That there are often considerable difficulties about identifying the precise nature and scope of certain traditions, even such singularly prominent ones as the Zion tradition of Jerusalem, must also remain a factor to be borne in mind. Thus, for example, how far the Zion tradition was oriented towards all Israel, rather than only to the city of Jerusalem or the kingdom of Judah, and how it was related to the tradition of Yahweh's conflict with the nations and the claim of the Davidic dynasty to kingship over all Israel, are all questions in which further discussion and clarification is desirable. We cannot proceed with a study of the use of tradition in the prophets on the assumption that each tradition itself was a closely defined and well-known entity. Thus it is often exceedingly difficult to ascertain how far a prophet was deliberately modifying a tradition, or whether the apparent novelty in his use of it has arisen because of the modified form in which the prophet received the tradition. Even more complex is the question whether on occasion a later prophet is consciously alluding to an earlier pronouncement of another prophet or whether both have drawn on elements of a common tradition.[1] In considering the questions which arise here we can only endeavour to keep in mind the variety of ways in which traditions can be reflected in prophecy.

Just as there are problems about the precise delineation of the nature and scope of certain traditions, so also there are many uncertainties concerning the exact setting to which a tradition is to be ascribed. It is a fundamental feature of H. Gunkel's *Gattungsgeschichte* that each *Gattung*, or type, has a particular setting in life. Yet this cannot be applied too rigidly, and it becomes evident that certain types, or forms, of speech and literature were located in more than one setting. This particularly applies to certain didactic forms where the teaching situation which is presupposed

[1] An example of this problem may be seen in Mic. 5:3, where it is possible that an allusion is intended to the Immanuel prophecy of Is. 7:14. Alternatively it is arguable that both prophecies have arisen independently by reference to a widely known tradition.

by the type may be one of several kinds. Thus it is possible to maintain that the setting of such teaching activity was the family, the schoolroom, the royal court, or even the synagogue in each of which certain types of religious and moral instruction were given. Thus the problem of identifying the background and setting of what have been regarded as wisdom traditions and forms of speech becomes very acute, and often no clear and final conclusions can be drawn which would enable us to trace how wisdom influence was felt by the prophets. In many cases so-called 'wisdom' forms would appear to be little more than rhetorical devices or homiletical aids with no clear setting or exclusive attachment to any one professional, social, or religious group. It is not clear that the 'wise' in Israel formed a separate and recognizable circle, or that prophetic and wisdom circles were sufficiently independent and separately identifiable groups so as to enable us to mark the boundaries between them. The implications as to the significance of the prophetic use of traditional features elsewhere associated with wisdom are then very far from obvious, or easily decided. Hence, we must guard against pressing the significance of certain features with traditional associations which are to be found in the prophetic literature in a way which overshadows the clear statements of the text. Inferences are seldom as certain as the facts from which they are deduced, and the recognition of this aspect of method is important if progress is to be made along form-critical and traditio-historical lines. The constant need to be prepared to reassess the nature of forms and traditions must be upheld.

In line with this question of method the familiar problems of identifying secondary material in the prophetic literature must be recalled. As we have seen in regard to the prophetic concern with the tradition of the Sinai covenant and its law, material which apparently refers to these in Amos and Hosea is usually, and rightly, regarded as secondary. Yet such material has now become part of the explicit context of the passages concerned, and must be treated with the utmost seriousness. It reveals, however imperfectly, a world of theological interpretation and assessment which accompanied the preservation of these prophecies. The tradition of the Sinai covenant therefore appears as important in the redaction and later use of these prophecies, even though it appears that in their own words the original prophets made no explicit reference to it. From such clues we can begin to unravel a significant theology of prophecy which viewed it against certain ideas of covenant which flourished most of all in the Deuteronomic school. In a remarkable way the figure of the prophet became stereotyped and coloured to form a part of the tradition of the covenant. How far certain prophets themselves contributed to the formulation of this remarkable, and very central, Deuteronomic theology of covenant is still not entirely clear. The prophet certainly became a figure viewed as the bearer and representative of a particular tradition in a way that became both influential and widely known. That the prophetic corpus in the Old Testament canon owed much to this tradition about prophecy is not in doubt.

This factor of the emergence of certain traditions in the Old Testament about the nature and role of prophecy raises also the range of problems concerning the distinction between the influence of prophetic and non-prophetic traditions upon the prophets. Perhaps in some ways the distinction is a rather fine one, but it is not altogether without significance. Most directly the type of traditio-historical investigation which we have been considering concerns the study of how religious traditions from outside the circle of prophecy influenced individual prophets. Yet alongside this it has become evident that some prophets reveal a strong familiarity with the work of their prophetic predecessors. Thus it has been widely accepted that Isaiah was influenced by Amos, Jeremiah by Hosea, and it has been argued that Ezekiel in particular shows a marked familiarity with a long line of prophetic predecessors.[2] We must certainly include these features in any study of prophecy and tradition, and it is noteworthy that in some aspects, as for example the prophetic call-narratives, our preserved accounts of the prophets' experiences have been strongly influenced by elements of a distinctively prophetic tradition. We can therefore see in this shaping of material in line with a distinctively prophetic pattern a further factor which contributed to the formation of a well-defined tradition about the nature and role of the prophets in Israel. Further consequences of this are certainly to be seen in the peculiar features of the Jeremiah tradition.

Finally, we may raise the question of what is at stake in this very diversified discussion about the prophets and tradition. Essentially the answer must lie in the area of a deeper understanding of the nature of divine revelation. That prophecy, familiar as a widespread religious phenomenon, reached a remarkable peak of insight and value as an agency of communion between man and God in ancient

[2] W. Zimmerli, *Ezechiel* (BKAT XIII, 1), I, pp. 66 ff.

GP

Israel is readily apparent to all who are familiar with the Judaeo Christian tradition. Hence, we must inquire how prophecy wa experienced, and what it mediated by way of revelation. It is al too easy to explain prophecy as an eruption of the divine spirit hidde in the inner recesses of the spirit of man. On such a basis it i perhaps less significant what was communicated than the fac that such communication has taken place, evidencing as it doe the presence of God's spirit in man. The fact of God's communio with men would thereby be more forcibly shown than by an doctrinal assessment of its possibility. Yet, in fact, we know all to little of the psychological processes which relate to the experienc of prophetic inspiration, and the age-old problem of false prophec amply attests the immense importance of the message as well a the spirit of prophecy. The prophets themselves focused thei claim to be God's spokesmen upon the truthfulness of the message they brought. We can only examine and understand this claim b placing the prophetic words in the historical context of thought an religious life in which they were given. This amounts to an attemp to see the prophetic words in the light of the tradition which formed their background. This is not to deny to the prophet their rightful originality, but to endeavour to see clearly where tha originality lay, and to seek to understand how the subjectiv experience presupposed by the claim that God had spoken t them was related to an objective world of ideas and institution The relationship of the prophets to tradition, therefore, may b regarded as a particular aspect of the question of the nature an possibility of divine revelation, viewed in regard to the prophets c the Old Testament. It thus provides a significant point of contac and common interest between the theological concerns of th biblical scholar and the wider investigation of the nature an history of mankind's religious experience.

Select Bibliography

THE PROPHETS AND THE COVENANT

K. Baltzer, *The Covenant Formulary*, Oxford, 1972.

W. Brueggemann, 'Amos 4:4–13 and Israel's Covenant Worship', *VT* 15 (1965), pp. 1–15.

W. Brueggemann, *Tradition for Crisis. A Study in Hosea*, Richmond, 1968.

R. E. Clements, *Prophecy and Covenant* (SBT 43), London, 1965,

F. C. Fensham, 'Clauses of Protection in the Hittite Treaties and in the Old Testament', *VT* 13 (1963), pp. 133–43

F. C. Fensham, 'Common Trends in Curses of the Near Eastern Treaties and *Kudurru*-Inscriptions Compared with Maledictions of Amos and Isaiah', *ZAW* 75 (1963), pp. 155–75.

F. C. Fensham, 'Maledictions and Benedictions in Ancient Near-Eastern Vassal Treaties and the Old Testament', *ZAW* 74 (1962) pp. 1–19.

F. C. Fensham, 'Covenant, Promise and Expectation in the Bible'. *ThZ* 23 (1967), pp. 305–22.

F. C. Fensham, 'Father and Son as Terminology for Treaty and Covenant', *Near Eastern Studies in Honor of W. F. Albright*, ed. H. Goedicke, Baltimore, 1971, pp. 121–35.

F. C. Fensham, 'A Possible Origin of the Concept of the Day of the Lord', *Proceedings of the Ninth Meeting of Die Ou-Testamentiese Werkgemeenschap in Suid-Afrika*, 1966, pp. 90–7.

B. Gemser, 'The *rib*- or Controversy-Pattern in Hebrew Mentality' *Adhuc Loquitur*, Leiden, 1968, pp. 116–37.

J. Harvey, 'Le "*rîb* pattern" requisitoire prophétique sur la rupture de l'alliance', *Biblica* 43 (1962), pp. 172–96.

J. Harvey, 'Le plaidoyer prophétique contre Israël après la rupture de l'alliance', Paris-Montreal, 1967.

J. Hempel, 'Die israelitischen Anschauungen von Segen und Fluch im Lichte altorientalischer Parallelen', *APOXYSMATA* (BZAW 81), 1961, pp. 30–113.

D. R. Hillers, *Treaty Curses and the Old Testament Prophet.* (Biblica et Orientalia 16), Rome, 1964.

D. R. Hillers, *Covenant. The History of a Biblical Idea*, Baltimore 1969.

D. R. Hillers, 'A Note on Some Treaty Terminology in the Old Testament', *BASOR* 176 (1964), pp. 46–7.

F. Horst, 'Segen und Segenshandlungen in der Bibel', *Gotte. Recht* (ThB 12), Munich, 1961, pp. 188–202.

H. B. Huffmon, 'The Treaty Background of Hebrew *Yada*'', *BASOR* 181 (1966), pp. 31–7.

H. B. Huffmon, and S. B. Parker, 'A Further Note on the Treaty Background of Hebrew *Yada*'', *BASOR* 184 (1966), pp. 36–8

H. B. Huffmon, 'The Covenant Lawsuit in the Prophets', *JBL* 78 (1959), pp. 285–95.

H. J. Kraus, *Die prophetische Verkündigung des Rechts in Israe.* (ThSt 51), Zürich, 1957.

N. Lohfink, S.J., 'Hate and Love in Osee 9:15', *CBQ* 25 (1963) p. 417.

D. J. McCarthy, 'Hosea 12:2. Covenant by Oil', *VT* 14 (1964) pp. 215–21.

D. J. McCarthy, 'Notes on the Love of God in Deuteronomy and the Father-Son Relationship between Yahweh and Israel', *CBQ* 72 (1965), pp. 144–7.

D. J. McCarthy, *Old Testament Covenant. A Survey of Curren. Opinions*, Oxford, 1972.

W. L. Moran, 'A Note on the Treaty Terminology of the Sefire Stelas', *JNES* 22 (1963), pp. 173–6.

W. L. Moran, 'The Ancient Near Eastern Background of the Love of God in Deuteronomy', *CBQ* 25 (1963), pp. 77–87.

F. L. Moriarty, 'Prophets and Covenant', *Gregorianum* 66 (1965) pp. 817–33.

J. Muilenburg, 'The Form and Structure of the Covenanta Formulations', *VT* 9 (1959), pp. 347–65.

J. Muilenburg, 'The "Office" of the Prophet in Ancient Israel' *The Bible in Modern Scholarship*, ed. J. P. Hyatt, Nashville 1965, pp. 74–79.

L. Perlitt, *Bundestheologie im Alten Testament* (WMANT 36) Neukirchen, 1969.

H. Graf Reventlow, *Das Amt des Propheten bei Amos* (FRLANT 80), Göttingen, 1962.

H. Graf Reventlow, 'Prophetenamt und Mittleramt', *ZThK* 58 (1961), pp. 269–84.

H. Graf Reventlow, *Liturgie und prophetisches Ich bei Jeremia*, Gütersloh, 1963.

H. Graf Reventlow, *Wächter über Israel. Ezechiel und seine Tradition* (BZAW 82), Berlin, 1962.

E. A. Schächter, 'Bundesformular und prophetischer Unheilspruch', *Biblica* 48 (1967), pp. 128–31.

M. Sekine, 'Davidsbund und Sinaibund bei Jeremia', *VT* 9 (1959), pp. 47–57.

R. Smend, *Die Bundesformel* (ThSt 68), Zürich, 1963.

E. von Waldow, *Der traditionsgeschichtliche Hintergrund der prophetischen Gerichtsreden* (BZAW 85), Berlin, 1963.

G. E. Wright, 'The Lawsuit of God. A Form-Critical Study of Deuteronomy 32', *Israel's Prophetic Heritage* (eds. B. W. Anderson and W. Harrelson), London, 1962, pp. 26–67.

W. Zimmerli, *The Law and the Prophets*, Oxford, 1965.

TRADITION AND THE PROPHETIC CONSCIOUSNESS

M. Buber, *The Prophetic Faith*, New York, 1949.

I. Engnell, 'Profetia och Tradition. Några synpunkter på ett gammaltestamentligt centralproblem', *SEÅ* 12 (1947), pp. 94–123.

I. Engnell, 'Prophets and Prophetism in the Old Testament', *Critical Essays on the Old Testament*, London, 1970, pp. 123–79.

G. Fohrer, *Introduction to the Old Testament*, London, 1970.

G. Fohrer, '"Tradition und Interpretation im Alten Testament', *Studien zur alttestamentlichen Theologie und Geschichte* (1949–1966) (BZAW 115), Berlin, 1969.

G. Fohrer, 'Remarks on Modern Interpretation of the Prophets', *JBL* 80 (1961), pp. 309–19.

G. Fohrer, 'Die Propheten des Alten Testaments im Blickfeld neuer Forschung', *Studien zur alttestamentlichen Prophetie und Geschichte (1949–1966)*, pp. 1–17.

M. L. Henry, *Prophet und Tradition. Versuch einer Problemstellung* (BZAW 116), Berlin 1969.

R. Knierim, 'The Vocation of Isaiah,' *VT* 18 (1968), pp. 64–8.

J. Lindblom, *Prophecy in Ancient Israel*, Oxford, 1962.

S. Mowinckel, *Prophecy and Tradition. The Prophetic Books in the Light of the Study of the Growth and History of the Tradition*, Oslo, 1946.

N. W. Porteous, 'The Prophets and the Problem of Continuity', *Living the Mystery*, Oxford, 1967, pp. 113–26.

R. Rendtorff, 'Tradition und Prophetie', *Theologia Viatorum* VIII, Berlin, 1962, pp. 216–26.

J. Vollmer, *Geschichtliche Rückblicke und Motive in der Prophetie des Amos, Hosea and Jesaia*, Berlin, 1971 (BZAW 119).

G. Widengren, *Literary and Psychological Aspects of the Hebrew Prophets*, Uppsala, 1948.

THE ROLE OF THE PROPHET
ACCORDING TO ISRAELITE TRADITION

P. R. Ackroyd, 'Aspects of the Jeremiah Tradition', *Indian Journal of Theology* 20 (1971), pp. 1–12.

J. L. Crenshaw, *Prophetic Conflict. Its Effect upon Israelite Religion* (BZAW 124), Berlin, 1971.

F. Crüsemann, 'Kritik an Amos im deuteronomistischen Geschichtswerk. Erwägungen zu 2. Könige 14, 27', *Probleme Biblischer Theologie* (von Rad Festschrift), Munich, 1971, pp. 57–63.

O. Eissfeldt, 'Amos und Jona im volkstümlicher Überlieferung', *Kleine Schriften* IV, Tübingen, 1968, pp. 137–42.

S. Herrmann, *Die prophetischen Heilserwartungen im Alten Testament* (BWANT V:5), Stuttgart, 1965.

S. Herrmann, *Prophetie und Wirklichkeit in der Epoche des babylonischen Exils* (Arbeiten zur Theologie 1:32), Stuttgart, 1967.

S. Herrmann, 'Die konstruktive Restauration. Das Deuteronomium als Mitte biblische Theologie', *Probleme Biblischer Theologie* (von Rad Festschrift), Munich, 1971, pp. 155–70.

U. Kellermann, 'Der Amosschluss als Stimme deuteronomistischer Heilshoffnung' *EvTh* 29 (1969), pp. 169–83.

G. C. Macholz, 'Jeremia in der Kontinuität der Prophetie', *Probleme Biblischer Theologie* (von Rad Festschrift), Munich, 1971, p. 306–34.

A. Jepsen, 'Gottesmann und Prophet. Anmerkungen zum Kapitel I Könige 13', *Probleme Biblischer Theologie* (von Rad Festschrift), Munich, 1971, pp. 171–82.

E. W. Nicholson, *Preaching to the Exiles*, Oxford, 1971.

G. von Rad, 'The Deuteronomistic Theology of History in the Books of Kings, *Studies in Deuteronomy* (SBT 9), London, 1953, pp. 74–91.

C. Rietzschel, *Das Problem der Urrolle. Ein Beitrag zur Redaktionsgeschichte des Jeremiabuches*, Gütersloh, 1966.

W. H. Schmidt, 'Die deuteronomistische Redaktion des Amosbuches, *ZAW* 77 (1965), pp. 168–93.

O. H. Steck, *Israel und das gewaltsame Geschick der Propheten* (WMANT 23), Neukirchen, 1967.

H. J. Stoebe, 'Überlegungen zu den geistlichen Voraussetzungen der Prophetie des Amos', *Wort-Gebot-Glaube* (W. Eichrodt Festschrift) (ATANT 59), ed. H. J. Stoebe, Zürich, 1970, 209–25.

G. Wanke, *Untersuchungen zur sogenannten Baruchschrift* (BZAW 122), Berlin, 1971.

I. Willi-Plein, *Vorformen der Schriftexegese innerhalb des Alten Testaments. Untersuchungen zum literarischen Werden der auf Amos, Hosea und Micha zurückgehenden Bücher im hebraischen Zwölfprophetenbuch* (BZAW 123), Berlin, 1971.

H. W. Wolff, 'Hoseas geistige Heimat', *Gesammelte Studien zum A. T.* (ThB 22), Munich, 1964, pp. 232–50.

H. W. Wolff, *Hosea* (BKAT XIV, 1), 2nd ed. Neukirchen, 1965.

H. W. Wolff, *Joel und Amos* (BKAT XIV, 2), Neukirchen, 1969.

H. W. Wolff, 'Das Ende des Heiligtums in Bethel', *Archäeologie und altes Testament* (K. Galling Festschrift), Tübingen, 1970, 287–98.

THE PROPHETS AND THE NATIONS

A. Bentzen, 'The Ritual Background of Amos i.2–ii. 16', *Oudtestamentische Studien* VIII, Leiden, 1950, pp. 85–99.

B. S. Childs, *Isaiah and the Assyrian Crisis* (SBT Second Series 3), London, 1967.

S. Erlandsson, *The Burden of Babylon. A Study of Isaiah* 13:2–14: 23 (Coniectanea Biblica O.T. Series 4), Lund, 1970.

N. K. Gottwald, *All the Kingdoms of the Earth. Israelite Prophecy and*

International Relations in the Ancient Near East, New York, 1964.

H. Gunkel 'Einleitung. Die grosse Propheten. Die Schriften des A.T.' II/2, 2. Aufl. 1923, pp. ix–lxx.

J. H. Hayes, 'The Usage of Oracles against Foreign Nations in Ancient Israel', *JBL* 87 (1968), pp. 81–92.

F. Hesse, 'Würzelt die prophetische Gerichtsrede im israelitischen Kult?', *ZAW* 65 (1953), pp. 45–53.

G. H. Jones, *An Examination of Some Leading Motifs in the Prophetic Oracles against Foreign Nations*, Dissertation, University of Wales, 1970.

O. Kaiser, *Isaiah 1–12* (Old Testament Library), London, 1972.

H. M. Lutz, *Jahwe, Jerusalem und die Völker. Zur Vorgeschichte von Sach. 12.1–8 und 14, 1–5* (WMANT 27), Neukirchen, 1968.

R. Martin-Achard, *A Light to the Nations*, Edinburgh, 1962.

W. L. Moran, 'New Evidence from Mari on the History of Prophecy', *Biblica* 50 (1969), pp. 15–56.

A. Malamat, 'Prophetic Revelations in New Documents from Mari and the Bible', *Geneva Congress Volume* (SVT XV), Leiden, 1966, pp. 214–19.

H.–P. Müller, *Ursprünge und Strukturen alttestamentlicher Eschatologie* (BZAW 109), Berlin, 1969.

F. Stoltz, *Strukturen und Figuren im Kult von Jerusalem. Studien zur altoreintalischer vor- und frühisraelitischen Religion* (BZAW 118), Berlin, 1970.

R. de Vaux, 'Jerusalem and the Prophets', *Interpreting the Prophetic Tradition*, New York-Cincinnati, 1969, pp. 275–300.

Th. C. Vriezen, 'Essentials of the Theology of Isaiah', *Israel's Prophetic Heritage* (eds. W. Harrelson and B. W. Anderson), London, 1962, pp. 128–46.

E. Würthwein, 'Der Ursprung der prophetischen Gerichtsrede', *Wort und Existenz*, Göttingen, 1970, pp. 111–26.

E. Würthwein, 'Amos—Studien', *Wort und Existenz*, pp. 68–110.

E. Würthwein, 'Jesaja 7,1–9. Ein Beitrag zu den Thema: Prophetie und Politik', *Wort und Existenz*, pp. 127–43.

WISDOM, PROPHECY, AND APOCALYPTIC

J. L. Crenshaw, 'The Influence of the Wise upon Amos. The "Doxologies of Amos" and Job 5:9–16; 9:5–10', *ZAW* 79 (1967), pp. 45–52.

J. Fichtner, 'Jesaja unter den Weisen', *Gottes Weisheit*, ed. K. D. Fricke, Stuttgart, 1965, pp. 18–26.

J. Fichter, 'Jahwes Plan in der Botschaft des Jesaja', *Gottes Weisheit*, pp. 27–43.

G. Fohrer, 'Die Weisheit im Alten Testament', *Studien zur alttestamentlichen Theologie und Geschichte* (1949–1966) (BZAW 115), Berlin, 1969, pp. 242–74.

B. Gemser, 'The Spiritual Structure of Biblical Aphoristic Wisdom', *Adhuc Loquitur*, Leiden, 1968, pp. 138–49.

E. Gerstenberger, 'The Woe-Oracles of the Prophets', *JBL* 81 (1962), pp. 249–63.

E. Gerstenberger, *Wesen und Herkunft des 'apodiktischen Rechts'* (WMANT 20), Neukirchen, 1965.

R. Gordis' 'The Social Background of Wisdom Literature', *Poets, Prophets and Sages*, Indiana, 1971, pp. 160–97.

J. Lindblom, 'Wisdom in the Old Testament Prophets', *Wisdom in Israel and the Ancient Near East* (H. H. Rowley Festschrift) (SVT III), Leiden, 1955. pp. 192–204.

W. McKane, *Prophets and Wise Men* (SBT 44), London, 1965.

A. Malamat, 'Organs of Statecraft in the Israelite Monarchy', *BA* 28 (1965), pp. 34–65.

R. E. Murphy, 'Form Criticism and Wisdom Literature', *CBQ* 31 (1969), pp. 475–83.

G. von Rad, *Old Testament Theology*, Vol. II, Edinburgh, 1965.

G. von Rad, *Wisdom in Israel*, London, 1972.

H. H. Schmid, 'Amos. Zur Frage nach der "geistige Heimat" des Propheten', *Wort und Dienst*, N.F. 10 (1969), pp. 85–103.

R. B. Y. Scott, *The Way of Wisdom*, New York, 1971.

S. Terrien, 'Amos and Wisdom', *Israel's Prophetic Heritage*, pp. 108–15.

H. W. Wolff, *Amos' geistige Heimat* (WMANT 18), Neukirchen, 1964.

Index of Authors